THE
OWNERS

A Titan's Guide To Building A Limitless Agency

Written and Compiled By:

Stephanie Dove Blake &
Franco Urbaez

To order more copies, go to TheOwnersBook.com

Named contributors have graciously agreed to publish their work in this compilation, giving full rights to use the contents of their submission for marketing and informational purposes.

Cover designed by Dream Big Media

Typesetting by Kathy Miiller, TRU Consulting

Selected icon graphics sourced with permission from www.flaticon.com

ClickFunnels® is a trademark of Etison LLC.
Google® is a trademark of Google, Inc.
Facebook® is a trademark of Facebook, Inc.
Instagram® is a trademark of Instagram, LLC.
Voxer® is a registered trademark of Voxer IP, LLC
WordPress®, Zapier®, IFTTT®, Lyft®, PowerBars®, and SLACK® are registered trademarks of their respective organizations

Published by Social Sparrow Publishing
Anna, TX USA

ISBN: 979-8-218-06234-7

V08272022

In a letter to Robert Hooke in 1675,
Isaac Newton made his most famous statement:
"If I have seen further, it is by standing on the shoulders of Giants."

Titan: A person or thing of very great strength, intellect, or importance.

As agency owners, if we want to be able to see further, it's important
to stand on the shoulders of Agency Titans who have walked the
path before us. The pages herein, contain EARNED wisdom that
comes from combined decades of agency experience.
So grab on, climb up, and take in the view.
There's a lot to learn and see from up here.

ACKNOWLEDGEMENTS

To Russell Brunson

It's actually super hard to write this acknowledgement because the gratefulness that I feel doesn't seem to be capturable in words. 7 years ago Russell Brunson didn't know me from Adam but as I sat in the seat at my first Funnel Hacking Live, he gave me the gift of BELIEF.

- Belief that I was an entrepreneur.
- Belief that I had a call on my life to serve a group of people.
- Belief that I could solve a big problem for the world and get paid well for doing it.
- Belief that I wasn't messed up, I was just an entrepreneur with no other entrepreneurs around me.

And those revelations were so impactful at the core of who I am today. Russell, it feels like I've said it a thousand times but from one visionary to another, thank you for choosing to show up for your 1% crazy tribe despite the journey being perilous and filled with obstacles. I believe the impact you've made has and will continue to make waves for generations to come. As a die-hard #funnelhacker, thank you!

To The Owners, The Contributors to This Book

To Hernan Vazquez, Steve J Larsen, Marley Jaxx, Preston Schmidli, McBilly Sy, Karen Sahetya, Damon Burton, Jason Feltman, Andrew Stickel, Nik Robbins, Dawn Sinkule, Andrea Peer, Erik Sorenson, Mia Paulus, Tyler Jorgeson and Mark Stern - THANK YOU!

When I thought of today's Agency Titans you all were the first to come to mind. I'm so thankful you made time to pour out your wisdom for this book with such an incredibly short deadline. You're all rockstars and humans that I'm so grateful to call friends. Rooting for you always!

DEDICATIONS

BY STEPHANIE DOVE BLAKE

John Blake. The love of my life, my own personal red-bearded superhero, the father of my beautiful children, and the seer of my soul. Without you, my agency wouldn't exist. Your love, support and insight were what truly built this agency - because without it, I might never have started. Thank you for saying "yes" that night 7 years ago to my hair-brained idea to reach out to a local chiropractor and ask him if I could run ads for him for free. I was scared, unsure, and lacked confidence but you never wavered. Thank you. I'll do this journey with you until the end of my days. I'm forever yours.

To my children, Josiah, Jude, Jossalyn and Journey... You were THE motivation that started it all. You're all so very precious and priceless to me and the thought of not being in your lives as you grew and learned was 100% not an option. Being your mother is the BIGGEST blessing of my life. I adore you all.

To my incredible Social Sparrow Team, I am so honored to have you. You are the ying to my yang and I couldn't do this without you all. I'm thankful for all of your heart, dedication, crazy mad skillz, and your dedication to providing for your family while being available to raise your kids. We work hard but we LOVE harder!

To Laura Couvillon, my biz bestie, friend and Integrator extraordinaire, thank you for walking this crazy journey with me. You have been so instrumental in my growth as an entrepreneur because you always bring a perspective that I couldn't see before. Your perspective, strategic brain, SUPER arranger skills, bio-hacking secrets, and 7 humor is all so PRICELESS. You're a god-send. Love you! #bettertogether

To Dr. Caleb Braddock, thank you for believing in this crazy, homeschooling momma of four with a bad back seven years ago. It's a privilege to do this work with you and call you friend.

DEDICATIONS

For Haylee, Grayson, Jemma, and Arrow.

The original Big Dreamers.

I love you more than words can say.

~ Franco

WHAT OTHERS ARE SAYING

"*The Owners* is the agency playbook I wish I had when I was first building my digital marketing agency for my fellow financial planners. The practical (and motivational) tips, strategies and plans truly are a goldmine, and as someone who's invested well over 6-figures in mentors, coaches and courses to achieve the level of success I have today, I can tell you, this book is like the cheatsheet to success (but you're not cheating!) When building a 7-figure (or more) agency, you have to master both the inner and outer game of entrepreneurship - mindset and action. The Owners gives you the winning playbook no matter what financial, emotional, relational or professional circumstance you are currently in. There is literally no excuse for not achieving success in your agency (and life) after reading this book."

Dr. Portia R. Jackson, CFP®
Wealth Coach for 7-Figure Entrepreneurs

"I have now read this book multiple times and the wisdom and tips in here reach far beyond agency owners; they are TRANSFORMATIONAL TRUTHS for business in general. As a business consultant who has worked with global industry leaders and in management for about 30 years, I know that many of these SECRETS TO SUCCESS given by the contributors are transformational. The contributors are open and authentic about their mistakes and generous with their advice. I highly recommend purchasing one for each of your leadership team. What they shared is not business theory or complex processes, but simple, practical and proven practices that the best in business live and thrive by using."

Kevin Miiller, PE, MBA
Founder, ITCB Business Consulting

"As I was reading I was amazed by how much wisdom and experience they had compiled into one book. Nothing was held back. It's inspiring, easy to read, and makes you want to take action. If you are an agency owner, no matter what stage you are, you need to read this book. It will shortcut time, effort and money."

Gonzalo Jimenez
Founder & Tech Strategist at WeBuildFunnels.Pro

"The challenge I had with this book is not mining the gold to apply in my work but instead picking one thing out of the treasure trove in these pages to implement first. What I love most about this book is that you get real people with real life stories that share what really works. These titans who run these massive agencies let you in on what makes a real difference in their business and how it can work for you too. If you run an agency or any business for that matter, I highly recommend this book."

Garrett Poole
President Fit Feat Inc.

"*The Owners* cuts through the BS and Hype to bring real actionable steps from respected industry experts. No fluff, real talk, real advice. If you are looking to start or grow your agency - you need this book."

Mae Cee
Lifestyle Brand Extraordinaire at Graphic Tee Academy

"Whether you're at the beginning of your agency journey or have spent a long time running down that road, The Owners is the encouragement and catalyst you need to see your agency's true potential.
This incredible collection of contributors transparently share the lessons and insights they've amassed from years of experiential learning, giving you the gift of actionable strategies you can start implementing today to take your agency to new heights. Grab a copy and a pen - you'll definitely want to take notes!"

Kari Poppleton
Operations & Marketing Measurement Consultant

"Reading The Owners is like being a fly on the wall of a mastermind for agency owners. Stephanie truly has a gift for gathering great minds and getting the best out of them. It's a rare and beautiful thing to hear the raw and real stories from agency owners who've persevered and proven that with the right community and a little bit of crazy, amazing things can happen."

Matt Deseno
8 Figure Agency Owner

Contents

PREFACE

When Franco and I (Stephanie) sat down to figure out how to best extract gold from the minds and hearts of the Agency Titans, we determined that the secrets lie in their answers to 4 questions:

▶ What was the greatest piece of advice you received from a mentor or coach that made the biggest impact in your agency journey?

▶ What would you say was the biggest contributing factor to your success?

▶ What is the greatest skill you needed to develop to be as successful as you are?

▶ What was the greatest mindset or identity shift you had to have to be as successful as you are?

These 4 questions were crafted to pull out the best of the best advice from people who have walked this path before. At first I was skeptical about using this format but Franco was so convinced and excited about it that I leaned in and said, "Ok, let's prove it and ask ourselves these questions and see what comes out."

So we did. As the answers poured out of each of us, one by one, we knew we had hit the right "gold digging pick," if you will, to mine GOLD.

In the chapters that follow you will read a brief intro from each Agency Titan followed by their answers to each of the questions. In the pages that follow, you will find GOLD from Agency Titans that applies to every phase of the journey, from starting to growth to leadership and beyond

At the end of each chapter, you will find a page to record the GOLD that you cultivated from what was shared. Have you ever noticed that when you watch a great movie for a second and third time you walk away with little details you never saw before? Well, the GOLD in these pages works in much the same way. Based on your circumstances right now, you will find solutions and encouragement. Next time you read it, you will pull out deeper nuggets that never resonated before. Use this book as a tool, an inspiration and encouragement in your journey. Come back to it often and hear the words of those who have been through the fire and come out on top. Our hope is that their advice will lead you to greater success in a shorter time.

From Franco and I, please challenge yourself to consume this book but don't leave it on the shelf. We believe it can be a catalyst for growth for you as the .05% crazy owners.

Consume and Take Action, my friends! We're rooting for you!

PS - If you find value in this book (which I'm betting you will), please go to Amazon and drop us a review so that we can help get this book in the hands of more agency owners.

INTRODUCTION

Agency life is not for the faint of heart. It's for a special breed of entrepreneur, and if this book is in your hands, I'm betting you're a member of that small sub-group called *agency owners* that are a tad crazier than the average entrepreneur. Russell Brunson often calls entrepreneurs the 1% crazy of the world…because we're crazy enough to believe we can change the world. And I agree with him.

I also propose that we the Agency Owners make up a smaller .05% crazy, because we're just crazy enough to serve the 1% crazy with our agency services

→ Grit.

→ Determination.

→ Emotional Intelligence.

→ Fearlessness.

→ Risk Tolerance.

→ A Strategic Mind.

→ Intuitive Instincts.

→ Unwavering Dedication.

→ Foresight.

→ Diligence.

→ Tenacity with a Touch of Bull-Headedness.

It takes an extra dose of ALL of that to serve entrepreneur visionaries.

And that's you, agency owner! The .05% CRAZIER!

When I first started my agency, I had no idea that the things on that list were all there within me. I had the advantage of being so incredibly hungry, plus my back was against a wall. It was DO or let my dreams DIE (e.g., homeschooling my out-of-the-box children). It was a wild ride, and I'll share more about how a high school DROPOUT, homeschooling momma of four built a 7-figure agency from scratch while working a full-time job later in this book.

If I can do it, SO. CAN. YOU.
YOU are the reason this book exists.

When Russell Brunson asked me to speak at Funnel Hacking Live (FHL), the first thing I remember was the weight of the honor to get to speak to my fellow die-hard #funnelhackers.

(Actually, that's the 2nd thing… the 1st thing I remember was standing there, staring at Voxer®, not being able to process what I was hearing Russell say. I listened again. Nope… still not processing.)

I literally felt like I needed to pinch myself.

Once I regained composure and my kids stopped screaming with me, I started sorting through every piece of GOLD I've picked up over the years, trying to prepare for my talk. There was just so much! I've spent multiple 6-figures investing in my brain via masterminds and courses.

What were the most important things to share?

What would make the biggest impact?

What would deliver BELIEF paired with strategy with a touch of *game-changing tactics…*?

Looking at the mountain of things I want to share, I realized it's much bigger than what I can possibly deliver in one hour on a stage at FHL. I began thinking about the **INCREDIBLE Agency Titans** that I've learned from over the years…

★ Billy Gene (my first agency mentor - love ya Billy!)
★ Robb Bailey
★ Nik Robbins
★ Dan Henry

These guys, along with the unstoppable Russell Brunson, were pivotal in my agency journey. Each one revealed game-changing keys that are with me in what I do in my agency to this day.

That's when it hit me: What if I could ask the best agency owners that I know to share their knowledge and wisdom with you?

And that leads us here. My hope is that this book serves as a cheat guide of sorts. The culmination of the hundreds of millions of dollars in revenue that has been generated by the contributors of this book is mind blowing but it's the *wisdom* they learned along the way that I want to give to you. Each of them went through the school of hard knocks OR they paid a mentor to get it.

I've asked each of them to give their BEST wisdom and advice for growing and scaling an agency. I hope you realize the value of the knowledge shared in this book and that it leads you to your very own game-changing breakthroughs.

Franco and I (Stephanie) compiled this book so that you could stand on the shoulders of Agency Titans.

Before I share what each of my agency mentors above gave me, I want to point out that I would have <u>NONE of these breakthroughs</u> if I hadn't chosen to pay to play. I *paid* to learn from those who had already walked the path and furthermore, I LISTENED and took *action* when they told me what to do. The entrepreneurial journey is hard and there's no reason to walk it alone.

★ Billy Gene ★

I still remember my first interview with Billy. I'd just had my first $7K day from a webinar to 10 chiropractors and I was flipping my lid. I could barely believe it. At that time the most I had ever made was $4K a month which seemed like I'd hit the jackpot. And there I was, $7K in ONE DAY.

It was 2016 and I was currently in Billy's original Clicks into Customers course. Just a month or so prior I had reached out to a local chiropractor to ask him if I could run ads for him for free. He very skeptically said yes and that month we blew up his practice. He was so impressed that he agreed to do a webinar with me for 10 of his chiropractic friends who lived all over the US. We did the webinar and much to my utter shock, I closed 9 out of 10 of the chiropractors that attended the webinar on a $2,000 package! WHAT?!

When I say I couldn't believe it guys, I really mean it. We were broke, living paycheck to paycheck, my husband was working 2 jobs, there were things in our house that were broken that we couldn't afford to fix, and we had never had that kind of money.

As I sat there, a chill went all the way to the bone at the thought of doing this all by myself. Nine new clients! I immediately remembered the mastermind that Billy Gene was trying to upsell everyone to. I picked up the phone and called Billy's team, told them what had happened, and that I was IN.

This was huge for me. I'd never bought a course before in my life. My initial course by Billy Gene had been paid for by a previous employer. At the time it was $997, and there was no way I could have paid for it, primarily because of my mental block, but also because we had no way of scraping together that amount of money.

Billy's team let him know about my $7K day, and being a smart marketer, Billy set up an interview with me. At the time I was trying to build my agency while homeschooling my four children. My kids were all pretty young at this time and I was trying desperately to figure out how to have this last minute interview with Billy and not have a kid bust in, yelling my name.

I decided to set up my computer in a seated bench window so I could pull the curtains around me, hopefully blocking out the noise, and effectively hiding me from view. That day I had 2 additional children in my home on top of my normal 4...so my efforts were futile.

Billy knew THEN what I only realized about 2 years later.

▶ **BREAKTHROUGH #1: Your customer is ALWAYS the hero. ALWAYS.**

In my interview with Billy, he began to tell me how to get more of what I had just tasted, and the answer was SYSTEMS and PROCESSES. He held up a HUGE binder with tons of little tabs on it and in typical Billy Gene style, said, "Our $h!t is no joke. These are the systems and processes that run our $h!t." He told me that I had to start documenting everything that I did so that I could easily teach new team members to do what I was doing.

▶ BREAKTHROUGH #2: Document EVERYTHING.

Boy, was he right. Within eight months I hired my first employee and because of Billy's advice, I was READY. I had made short videos documenting my processes and it was MAGIC.

To this day, systems and processes guide my agency, Social Sparrow, and I credit his advice, leadership and training as the reasons I was able to build so quickly.

★ Robb Bailey ★

Robb was a success story in Billy Gene's world because he had had a huge agency, but it wasn't profitable and he was overwhelmed with work. He was providing everything under the sun for his clients: websites, landing pages, ads, SEO and more. When he began working with Billy Gene, he had Robb niche down and provide ONE service. It changed the game for Robb.

Once I was down the agency road a bit, I started experiencing frustrating agency issues. I hired Robb and he connected me with his team. That's when I met Betsy. Robb talked about how incredible she was as his right-hand woman, and I saw it firsthand. Robb taught me many things, but two really stand out:

▶ BREAKTHROUGH #3. HIRE ROCKSTARS.
(Rockstars ≠ the most expensive hire you can find)

Betsy was an inspiration. She understood Robb. She understood the ads manager. She was a WHIZ, well spoken, detail oriented, and I just loved her. And she was home grown. She had no prior experience and highly valued being at home with her kids, so she started at a salary that was affordable to Robb as he trained her up. I needed a Betsy and I'd settle for no less. I learned to hire rockstars.

For me this meant finding moms like me who had skills to offer the world, yet prioritized being at home with their children. There's not one person on my team that started with prior knowledge of how to do their job. I hired for heart, character, and personality, and trained them from the ground up. Robb gave me the confidence to take action on this route and it has been one of the BEST decisions for me and my team. The part I love most is seeing kids and babies of these rockstar women on zoom as we're taking over the world!

▶ BREAKTHROUGH #4. DON'T MAKE IT COMPLICATED.

As I began to work with Robb and we'd have our coaching sessions, he made everything seem simple. It wasn't that everything *was* simple, it was that Robb refused to make things complicated. I would be in my head about a problem I was facing, and he'd cut through all the noise with one simple question and redirect my focus to the actual problem apart from "what-ifs."

I consider Robb Bailey a dear friend and he's still going and blowing today, making waves in the agency space.

★ Nik Robbins ★

Nik and I flew in the same circles for years. We'd see each other at conferences, and each time, Nik was climbing a new height. The thing that drew me to Nik was that he is a guy who genuinely cares.

▶ BREAKTHROUGH #5: Be a servant-leader with heart. (Make sure to read Nik's chapter in this book.)

He's not your typical coach/guru. He moves at the speed of light like the gurus, SELLS (like a beast) like the gurus, and is CONSTANTLY learning and improving himself like many of the guru. At the core, however, Nik is driven to make a difference and he hasn't lost touch with the fact that impact on a global scale, if it leaves a wake of hurting people in your path, isn't worth building.

While I learned a TON of valuable tactics, and grew as a saleswoman and entrepreneur while working with Nik, seeing him lead was the biggest lesson of all.

★ Dan Henry ★

Dan. Dan. Dan…. What can I say about Dan? (We all love Dan!) I can say that I'm incredibly thankful for Dan's part in my journey. I had the privilege of getting to watch his growth and his business blow up almost from the start.

I purchased Dan's course to refine my local business targeting tactics but what I gleaned from him was so much more. Dan was and is a BEAST. At the time he was building his empire, and I watched him push through what other people would perceive as limitations or boundaries, one after another.

One thing that mesmerized me about Dan was that he seemed to completely disregard other people's expectations of who he was or who he should be.

▶ **BREAKTHROUGH #6: Doing YOU is the BEST business strategy.**

This inspired me because as a somewhat bubbly, southern, unlikely agency owner, I had to learn to stop focusing on what I thought others thought of me. By showing up as my most authentic self in a male-dominated industry serving a male-dominated avatar (chiropractors), I stuck out like a sore thumb… in a good way. I brought a different feel to the "game" and did things differently and I wasn't afraid to let potential clients know it.

▶ **BREAKTHROUGH #7: Success rewards SPEED. Keep moving FORWARD… FAST.**

Dan taught me to move FAST and lean into my natural tendency to see no walls where others did. I threw caution to the wind and hit 6-figures in 6 months.

All of these Agency TITANS impacted my journey,
and there's SO MUCH MORE!

I wanted desperately to create this book for you but there was a kink in my plans. I didn't have this idea until we were 1.5 months out from

Funnel Hacking Live AND I hadn't even written my FHL talk yet + school was starting (a big deal with 4 kids) + we were moving + we were experiencing incredible growth in the agency.

How in the world was I going to be able to pull this off by myself? Enter Franco Urbaez to save the day! YOU (dear reader) are the reason this book exists as an idea, but Franco is the reason this book exists in your hands.

In 2019, I had the privilege of being asked to coach in Russell Brunson's 2CCX program which awakened my love of coaching. I coached 100's of entrepreneurs in multiple business industries, selling everything from running products, agency services and info products to selling vegan health and fitness. It was IN-CREDIBLE. Mind bending at times, but incredible.

A year later I started my own coaching business so that I could continue coaching on a much smaller scale while still running my agency. I took about 2-3 clients a quarter and it was invigorating! I watched two of my coaching clients go from literally ZERO to both hitting a million dollars in under 10 months. Talk about a wild ride.

Coaching will always be a part of what I do, so when Franco approached me at FHL 2021 and asked if I would be interested in being a guest coach in his agency program, The Limitless Agency, it was a literal no-brainer for me.

When I saw what Franco had built, I was in awe! His training on how to start an agency with NO ads... 100% organic is absolutely brilliant. He had done the work to lay out a framework for an entrepreneur to start, grow and SCALE an agency from beginning to end. Fast-forward to now, we've been coaching agency owners for about eight months together.

Franco is an Agency Titan and he knows what it takes to serve the 1% crazy. He gets it. That's why I'm so incredibly proud to be partnered with him to bring you this book-sized goldmine to life.

So this is your INVITATION:

Dive into this book with the mindset that ANYTHING is possible when you believe in yourself and you learn from Titans!

Mine the GOLD that's here for YOU in this book.

But don't just hold onto it...

DO SOMETHING with it!

Don't let FEAR keep you from fast action!

Find the gold and IMPLEMENT.

Move FORWARD at all costs.
(Except your family and your health)

Fail forward FAST so you can WIN faster.

And remember...

You NEVER lose. You only WIN or LEARN something.
(Paraphrased from Nelson Mandela)

I'm Rooting for YOU!

 Stephanie Dove Blake

The Owners

Chapter 1
Franco Urbaez

Franco Urbaez is a Christian. He is a husband to the most beautiful woman on earth, a father to 3 of the luckiest kids on earth, and a son of the Most High God. He also happens to be a successful, two-time 2 Comma Club award winning entrepreneur. Franco is the Founder of Dream Big Media, a marketing and consulting agency devoted to helping impact-driven entrepreneurs impact the world for good.

He is also the creator of Pepper, an automation software that has helped thousands of entrepreneurs grow their businesses organically by getting high-paying clients off of Facebook. Franco is the Creator of The Limitless Agency Mastermind, a coaching program that has helped over 100+ students successfully start and scale their agencies, many of them reaching 6 and 7-figure status.

Franco has built a global community of entrepreneurs with huge aspirations and even bigger hearts who call themselves, Big Dreamers. His mission is to help the big dreamers of the world take risks, defy the odds, achieve the impossible and ultimately change the world.

I was hiding away in my son's pitch-black room just staring at the ceiling. My 5 year old had fallen asleep already but I wasn't prepared to get up and face the world again... not yet.

My heart was pounding so hard I thought it might wake him up. I was lying there but I wasn't praying. I was doing the math in my head. *"How much longer could we go on like this? Was there anything I could sell? What would Haylee say when she found out we were going broke? How could I be so stupid? Who did I think I was?"* An idiot, that's what.

It had been 3 months since I quit my job as a warehouse worker, forfeiting benefits and a steady paycheck... all to chase a dream I was sure I would catch. I was determined to start up my very own marketing agency and grow it to 7 figures per year.

So as any recklessly optimistic entrepreneur would do, I liquidated my 401K plan. The grand total was $18,000. That was all the money I had saved slaving away 3 years of my life to make someone else rich...

And now, it was going to be my turn.

I had $18K in the bank when I left my job and 3 months later, we were down to about $5,000.

And it only got worse from there.

It took me just 4 months to lose everything I had...

With $0 in the bank and nothing coming in, all I had left was a few credit cards and a quickly fading hope that everything would eventually turn out alright. At the time, my wife and I couldn't scrape together $600 to fix our stovetop and microwave that broke down (we went without one for months).

But instead, using our credit cards as a lifeline, we threw a Hail Mary and bought a $1,000 ticket to attend a marketing event for the very first time.

Funnel Hacking Live.

And that's when everything changed. Attending that event was the weekend my life changed forever. I left inspired by the stories of aspiring entrepreneurs enduring the same struggles that I was facing myself. They shared eerily similar tales of sleepless nights when they were crippled with financial anxiety but somehow found the courage to push through when it would have been so easy to quit.

But more than just inspiration, I learned something that weekend... And what I learned saved me from shutting the doors to my marketing agency.

Over the course of the following 6 days, I committed to doing nothing else but implementing what I had learned from that event. And then, on the seventh day, I counted my spoils of war.

I couldn't believe it. I had done it!

I made $84,000... and I did it in 6 days.

I had earned more than my entire annual salary as a warehouse lead... in 6 days. And things just kept getting better. Our business continued to break new heights and set new records year after year.

We went on to win the coveted Two-Comma Club award from Clickfunnels...twice.

Success came easy and natural to me so long as I remembered to implement the principles I had learned from that event. In this chapter and surely throughout this book, you will discover some of these amazing business principles and strategies that have completely changed my life.

I started dead broke and over the last 5 years, I have gone on to make millions through the proper utilization of some of the strategies contained in this book.

That's impressive and all but what lights me up more is what my clients have accomplished. Over the last 3 years, I have helped hundreds of hopeful entrepreneurs start and scale marketing agencies, many of which have since scaled to 6 and 7 figures.

It has been the greatest privilege of my career to witness several of our clients leverage our teachings to start and grow their marketing agencies from nothing to well over $100,000 months.

Stephanie and I both have a deep love for coaching and a passion for seeing others win so it just made perfect sense for us to partner together and help marketing agencies grow to 7 figures within our Limitless Agency Mastermind. If you are interested in growing your marketing agency but want to avoid all of the painful mistakes and pitfalls most agency owners make when scaling, then schedule a call with a Limitless Agency Coach right here >> **www.golimitlessagency.com.**

What I share in the pages that follow, I consider to be the greatest lessons I have ever learned from my coaches, mentors, and my own personal life experiences in this crazy roller coaster ride we call entrepreneurship.

▶ **What was the greatest piece of advice you received from a mentor or coach that made the biggest impact in your agency journey?**

The greatest piece of advice I've ever received actually came from one of my agency clients, Blake Templeton. He was one of the strongest Christian men I've ever met and as a client, I had the privilege of jumping into weekly calls as he would coach up his leadership team in his real estate investment firm. Every single Wednesday, it would be all hands on deck for the Leadership Team Meeting which would last about 3-4 hours. I attended those calls for months and not once did we ever talk business during those meetings. Instead, he would empower and challenge each of us to our highest calling. Using biblical and real-world stories and illustrations, he would remind us of all of the unique talents, skills, and abilities God has given to each one of us. He would stretch us out of our comfort zones, calling on us to stand up and powerfully proclaim our identities in Christ. His thought process was that when his entire leadership team is firmly planted in their identities in Christ, they would be able to handle and overcome the complexities, stress, and uncertainties that inevitably come with trying to grow a billion-dollar brand. His circle of leaders needed to be able to operate at their highest potential, and not be confined to their current limitations.

The greatest piece of advice he gave me was one simple sentence that he drilled into me constantly. I would repeat it as a mantra throughout every day. It would cause me to do things I would never, ever do and it was the biggest catalyst to becoming the man that I am today, a man that I am proud of and have immense respect for.

That sentence was this: "If I can't, then I must!"

Your life is the sum of all of the decisions you've made up until this point. So whether you are pleased or frustrated with where your life is at today, the only person you can credit or blame is yourself. It's incredibly important then to understand just HOW you have come to make the decisions that you've made in your life that have brought you this far.

We make decisions based on our comfort zones. Anytime we are asked to do something that is outside of our comfort zone, negative emotions start to creep in. Anxiety, stress, worry, fear... These are natural reactions that your body produces in order to keep you "safe." It's your fight or flight response that is triggered when you consider taking a risk.

Your comfort zone keeps you safe, but you never grow in it. Growth always happens on the outside of your comfort zone. You are not the same person today as you were yesterday, you are always either growing or dying. Growing towards the potential of who you are supposed to become one day or coasting towards the end of your life. That's why I call your comfort zone the danger zone. What Blake instilled in me was that anytime I had an opportunity to grow closer to the man that I've always felt destined to become, even when my flesh vehemently fought against me to stay within the boundaries of my comfort zone, I had to push forward. If you feel like you can't do something, then you absolutely MUST do it. It is of paramount importance that you never let your flesh win by convincing you that something is impossible for you to do. Most of the time, the thing you think you can't do is not impossible, it's just uncomfortable. *"If I can't, then I must!"* is a life devoted to growth, forever striving to be more than you are today.

This one sentence has pushed me to try and accomplish things that in earlier stages of my life, I would have considered wildly out of reach. As a result of implementing "If I can't, then I must!" into every area of my life, I have built a business that has given me a life that I'm incredibly proud of.

Every single day, I know that by keeping true to this mantra, I am always growing closer to my potential and never allowing myself to be held back to what I think is possible for me. Taking on an "If I can't, then I must!" attitude has made anything and everything possible for me, and it can do the same for you.

▶ **What would you say was the biggest contributing factor to your success?**

The biggest contributing factor to my success has always been partnering with and learning from those who have already accomplished what I was trying to do. I remember learning this valuable lesson from Russell Brunson. When I was in one of his coaching programs years ago, I had the opportunity to fly out to a private event he held in Boise, Idaho called Traffic Secrets. This was a year before his book by the same name was published. He was testing his book material on us and it was mind-blowing stuff as usual. However, there was one day in particular on that trip that changed everything about how I was doing business, and how I was thinking about growing my own business. We visited ClickFunnels™ HQ and he led us into the infamous Inner Circle mastermind room where in one brief session, he shared one extremely valuable lesson that has made me millions and saved me countless hours and tons of stress.

When this concept finally clicked for me, in an instant, I went from being damn good at what I do to being one of the best in the world at what I do.

"It's not about the how, it's about the WHO."

Very likely, you've built (or are thinking about building) your business based on your own skill sets, the thing you're really good at. The truth is, you will never be the best in the world at that, because you are building a business. You see, for some people, ALL THEY ARE DOING is working on becoming the absolute BEST at their craft. They don't have to worry about building a business, marketing themselves, selling, delivery and fulfillment, building SOPs, hiring, managing and leading a team, scaling and so on... They are just focused on doing the thing they are really good at.

By building a business, you take yourself out of the running at becoming one of the best in the world at your craft. So instead of sacrificing sleep and time with your family so you can build the business AND still become one of the best in the world at your craft just so you can compete with someone who has an unfair advantage over you... hire them.

Imagine you wanted to start up a world-class restaurant, well there are two ways you could accomplish that. The first option would be to spend tens of thousands of dollars and several years to go to an elite culinary school so you could become a world-class chef.

Upon graduation, you would then build your restaurant and every night from there on, you would slave over the stove, cooking world class meals for hungry customers that walk in your door. That's one way you could build a world-class restaurant.

Or you could avoid years of schooling and open up right away by recruiting and hiring the best chefs in the world to come and work in your restaurant *for you*. You create an amazingly delightful experience for your hungry customers while your world class chefs are in the kitchen preparing the most exquisite meals of any restaurant in town.

Which restaurant owner would you rather be?

Once I learned this brilliant business hack of *"hiring the who"* instead of *"figuring out the how,"* I instantly began my quest to scour the earth and hunt for the highest quality talent I could find to work alongside me in my agency. I understood their needs, desires, goals, and ambitions and I made it my duty to help them achieve their dreams *within my company*. Once they believed that I truly had their best interests at heart, and they knew just how deeply I cared for them, I had a partner for life.

I shared the mission we had as a company of helping faith-based entrepreneurs achieve their big dreams with our world class marketing services. I shared with them my belief that the impact Dream Big Media would make in the lives and the businesses of the entrepreneurs we served would be our greatest opportunity to glorify God this side of Heaven.

It was because of our deeply ingrained culture and values within our organization that we were able to attract and partner with world class talent that allowed us to grow so quickly. Almost immediately these strategic partnerships blossomed into financial abundance. When talented people aligned with the same goals, missions and values that have distinct but necessary skill sets partner together to create something special, you experience explosive growth.

Partnering with and learning from experts, has hands down been the absolute number one strategy I have leveraged to accomplish way more than I ever could on my own in a fraction of the time that it would have taken me otherwise. This simple strategy is the exact reason why Stephanie and I created this book. When you stand on the shoulders of giants, their ceilings become your floor. In the hands of the right person, a business built on a foundation like that truly has no limits.

▶ **What is the greatest skill you needed to develop to be as successful as you are?**

A few years back, I watched in awe as one of my entrepreneurial heroes broke a world record. I remember having massive FOMO watching the aftermath of Russell Brunson having just finished presenting the world's greatest sales pitch from the biggest entrepreneurial stage of that time. News traveled lightning-fast throughout the internet marketing world, and I sat there in disbelief when it finally got to me. $3,000,000 in 90 minutes.

It took Russell Brunson just 90 minutes to meet and then influence an entire room to break out their wallets and throw their credit cards at him. I started to question everything I was doing in my life.

There I was charging hair salons a measly $500 per month for my marketing services and had to bend over backwards just to keep them paying, and Russell was making history earning millions from a stage in only 90 minutes of his time. It was then that I decided that I had to make a change. I vowed to do everything necessary to learn and master that skill no matter how long it took. And I still believe to this day that that resolution has been the greatest decision I've ever made in my entrepreneurial career.

Over the years, I've spent thousands of hours and have paid great sums of money to the best business and marketing minds in the world to master the art of selling one-to-many. During the height of the pandemic, I decided to host my very first in-person mastermind to put all of my hard work to the test.

24 marketing agencies flew in from all over the country to attend Big Dreamers Live, which was a 3-day event where I shared the actual, real-world strategies to scale your marketing agency to 7-figures. Each of them paid over $5,000 just to attend.

It was Dream Big Media's first ever event, it was my first time speaking in public in front of a live audience, and it was my first time going through the presentations I had prepared...*And we ended up breaking the industry record for the highest conversion rate at a live event!*

Living legends in the internet marketing space have told me that my conversion rate was even TOO high. That I must have been charging way too little...But it was a high-ticket offer: $18,000. And 23 out of the 24 people present at the event took action and signed up. That is a 95.8% conversion rate. (As far as I am aware, that is still the live event record for the highest conversion rate to a high-ticket offer!) We walked away from that event earning $411,000! That was pretty remarkable for a first-time event. I was blown away! So, how did we do it?

Yes it's true that there was a lot of wining and dining, there were fun activities and amazing food. But for all of the wonderful things we did to create an unforgettable event for our attendees, none of it was a deciding factor on why people bought. It took me several months to retrace my steps and unpack exactly what happened so that I could teach it in a way where others could achieve similar results...

But I did it. I could sum up the secrets of the success of that event into one simple sentence.

"If you can get the right offer in front of the right person with the right message at the right time, you will never have to worry about money ever again."

To craft a winning sales presentation, you need to have all 4 of these elements present. I knew that cracking the code on these 4 elements was the key to closing the entire room. Because it was my event, I was able to control almost all of the variables. Let me show you how I did it.

1. The Right Offer

I created an irresistible offer, giving them everything they needed and everything they THOUGHT they needed *(even if they didn't really need it)* to be successful. Read that again, it's important that you understand it. In preparing the offer, I asked myself this question, "Why would they NOT buy?" I knew that the answers were going to be either mindset/limiting beliefs or real, legitimate concerns.

Your offer overcomes the legitimate concerns, but your sales messaging overcomes your audience's limiting beliefs. People don't buy when they don't BELIEVE it will work. If they believed it would work, then they would buy. Your sales messaging instills BELIEF in their heart that this will work. Your offer then must convince their mind that *this can't fail.*

So to create the right offer that can sell out an entire room, you have to make your offer "FAIL-PROOF" in the mind of your prospect. And you do that by giving them everything they need to be successful and everything they think they will need to be successful *(even if they don't really need it).*

2. The Right Person

Not all money is created equal. A dollar from a dream client is worth $100 and a dollar from a nightmare client is worthless. Selling out the room is all about getting the right people in the room *(or on the phone)* in the first place. You want to be working with your dream clients, right?

So don't pitch to people who you KNOW aren't your dream clients. What if they say yes? Now you're indebted to working with someone you can't stand. What can be worse than that!?

I personally hand-picked every single person that I wanted to be at that event because I knew that those were my ideal, dream clients and that they were primed and ready to buy. I even made it a point to share that during my pitch. I told them all that they were hand-selected by me personally to be at that event. It's because I knew that I would be able to help every single one of them and also that working with them would be just awesome.

Make sure you are spending time finding and speaking to your dream clients: people you know you can help and that you would love to work with. It makes building your agency a million times easier and a heck of a lot more fun.

3. The Right Message

I knew that in order to prime my audience to buy from me at this event, they needed to undergo a complete and utter transformation. They needed to go from who they were when they walked in the door on that first day to becoming the person that would be ABLE to break through their comfort zones and pull the trigger when the opportunity to buy presented itself.

Knowing that, I crafted 7 key trainings designed to help them level up their mindset using powerful analogies and illustrations to persuade them to think differently about the things they once took for granted.

Slowly but surely, the attendees began to latch onto trustworthy sayings I was sharing with them that were designed to help them quickly grow in their mindset. When you are creating sales messaging designed to convert, it is not the "value-packed", step-by-step training that causes someone to buy. Transformation causes people to buy. When you shatter their limiting beliefs and replace them with certainty about a desirable outcome... that's when they'll buy.

Sure, you have to give them useful, practical strategies but the real, true, *treasured* value that causes your audience to empty their wallets for you comes from the mindset breakthroughs and identity shifts they undergo when hearing you speak.

Speak to their heart, not their mind.

4. The Right Time

This one is fairly simple to understand and implement. Most people never get very far with their marketing and sales because they fail to stay top of mind to their prospects. Don't quote me on these statistics but I've heard it said somewhere, that only about 10% of your prospects are ever ready to buy right now... All day long, everyone is fishing for those 10% who are ready to sign up today... but very few people ever even attempt to nurture the prospects who are ready to buy *soon*. Those business owners who devote time and attention and energy to consistently show up for their audience over the long-term never have to hunt for a sale.

Practice putting out content consistently to your audience and watch how famine turns to feast really quickly.

There are so many lessons to be learned from this one incredibly successful event that I literally do not have time enough to share it all with you in the scope of this chapter...Lucky for you, we recorded it. You can grab the entire event recordings for yourself (and if you want to catch the world-record presentation, it's called "The Fire or The Future"). Go here to grab the recordings:

>> **www.7trainings7figures.com**

I believe that the greatest business skill that any entrepreneur can learn is how to use the power of words and images to influence someone to take a desired course of action. It's developing the power of influence over another person or group of people to change their lives for the better - even when their own fight or flight mechanism is fighting hard to keep them firmly planted in their comfort zones.

It's a powerful skill that can get you whatever you want in life, if you just have the determination to develop and master it like I have.

▶ **What was the greatest mindset or identity shift you had to have to be as successful as you are? (Story, Practical Breakdown)**

The biggest mindset shift I had in my entrepreneurial journey came to me through one of my other mentors, Myron Golden.

I was at a Funnel Hacking Live event where several 2-Comma Club Award Winners each sat at a round table to answer questions and offer their invaluable advice. Attendees were given the opportunity to gather around, ask questions, listen and learn. Every 20 minutes or so, Dave Woodward would stand up on a table and blow a whistle, which meant that all of the listeners were to get up and move on to the next speaker. The problem was that whenever Dave blew the whistle, no one would leave Myron's table. His crowd just kept growing. I was sitting with my notebook at that round table listening to Myron for hours, writing pages and pages of notes. When I first sat down at Myron's round table, I was intrigued; but when I left, I was transformed.

In one 3-hour session, he single-handedly changed my entire perspective and relationship with money through the Bible. He showed me that I had a faulty understanding of what God had to say about money.

And it was because of that faulty understanding of money that I didn't have any. I was literally repelling it; my mindset kept me from being successful. As a Christian, I had always struggled and wrestled with what the Bible had to say about money. *"The love of money is the root of all evil."* (1 Tim 6:10, KJV) and *"No man can serve two masters: for either he will hate the one, and love the other; or you will be devoted to the one and despise the other. You cannot serve both God and money."* (Matt 6:24, ESV)

My desires to both honor God and, at the same time, be successful financially was a constant internal battle I struggled with.

How rich is too rich? At what point do you start making too much money that it jeopardizes your salvation? Just how poor am I supposed to be? Reading verses like these in the Bible always messed with my mind. It made me feel as though there was a correlation between being poor and being holy, or that being rich brought me out of favor with God. As a result, I was literally scared of making too much money. I was afraid of the man I could turn into if I ever became wealthy.

The more success I had, the more frightened I became that I was going to "lose myself." Myron helped me develop a good and real relationship with money. He showed me that money was just a tool, nothing more, nothing less. There are people out there in the world who become enslaved by it. Here is the ironic part: during my time of being "scared" of making money, all of that focus was actually making it an idol in my heart. It was a trap, because instead of focusing on serving and honoring God, I was focused on making sure I wasn't making too much or too little. Even though my desires were good, money, nevertheless, still became an idol to me.

Myron helped me realize that money is just a tool. It amplifies the person you already are. If you are generous with a little, you will be generous with a lot. If you're a jerk with a little, you'll be an even bigger jerk with a lot. You can probably think of people right now that fit the criteria in both camps. I think the point is to not serve money and become a slave to it, but rather to focus on serving God in the biggest and best way you possibly can with the talents He's gifted you with.

For me, it's building businesses. It's something I enjoy, something I'm passionate about, something I'm really good at. And when I focus on the clients I serve and helping them grow their businesses using my God-given talents, the money follows close behind.

Now, I no longer think of it. The money comes and goes, I have come to realize, none of it is mine anyway. It's all God's, I just happen to be a steward of it at any given point in time, trying my very best to earn as much as I can so that I can invest and give as much of it away for His Kingdom's sake. And that philosophy has taken me very far over the years. I hope this has helped you squash any limiting beliefs you have around making money as well. Make as much as you can so you have all the resources you need to make the biggest impact you can for the causes that are important to you

FrancoUrbaez.com

My Gold Nugget Takeaways

The Owners

Chapter 2
Marley Jaxx & Steve J Larsen

Hey, we are Steve J Larsen and Marley Jaxx. We help business owners who are struggling to get enough leads from paid ads to transform their YouTube channels into organic lead generation machines that deliver HOT LEADS ON DEMAND using our unique, YouTube Lead Machine 4 Step Framework.

Since we started our journey we've helped our clients double their leadflow while expanding their reach and revenue. Some of the most exponential growth has come from even the smallest YouTube channels! It's been a fun journey and in this chapter we want to share some of our insights and strategies with you.

There's money to make, minds to blow and socialism to smash!

▶ **What was the greatest piece of advice you received from a mentor or coach that made the biggest impact in your agency journey?**

We're both very lucky to count Alex and Lelia Hormozi as friends. They have an uncanny ability to get straight to the heart of an issue, diagnose the problem and offer real-world solutions almost instantly.

We happened to be at the same event in Texas and started talking about our companies (at the time we had separate businesses.) We outlined some of the projects we were working on and the ideas we had for new products and services.

Alex Hormozi started slow clapping....

"Amazing... brilliant... wow... you're both doing sooooo much stuff! I bet all of that will work out for ya! EVERYONE knows that going after lots of stuff is how you win…" (eye rolls)

Huh. We were getting sarcastically slow-clapped by Baby Thor and it was awkward. So we agreed to get rid of a few of our business ideas and pursuits but, "we'll just keep this one, and that one, and those over there."

The slow clapping started up again…

"Yeah… you're right… you do need to do alllllll this stuff… that's not going to burn you out! Go ahead… sounds amazzzzing!"

He then told us that we were splitting our focus in too many directions and dissipating our time and energy.

"You guys should join your companies and focus on ONE product!"

"But…"

SLOW CLAPPING AGAIN

"Ya great. I thought you guys were smart." No half-smile, or chuckles from him to relieve the pressure. He was serious.

We didn't know what to say. He was RIGHT! We both knew it but it's tough to change your thinking, especially when you've already put a lot of energy into a project.

Over the next few months, we both turned our active focus into consolidating and merging our companies. (Btw, it's pretty emotional to kill your biz-babies). We focused and got clear on providing ONE key result to the market…. turning 'ordinary' YouTube channels into powerful organic lead-generation machines… and we have just two methods of working with us: done-with-you or done-for-you.

It was a tough decision, but it was definitely the right move.

TAKEAWAY TIP: Are you "focusing" on too many projects or opportunities? What's the ONE offer you could smash if you put 100% of your time, attention, and focus on it?

What would you say was the biggest contributing factor to your success?

Systems.

When you know what your one big focus is, you then have to work out what systems are needed to generate the results consistently.

It's easy as an entrepreneur to get sucked into 'delivery' mode.

- Launching products.
- Coaching students.
- Building courses.
- Running events.
- And on and on…

But often, the answer we look for requires you to step back to create systems around the larger, strategic pieces of your company.

In the immortal words of Michael Gerber, you need to work 'on' your business as well as 'in' your business.

We broke our company into key areas: marketing and sales, done-with-you fulfillment, done-for-you fulfillment, finance, and admin, etc. We then worked out what all the key systems are that generate results in each of those areas. We actually sketched all core processes into flowchart drawn pictures. Once we had the systems, we made sure that we had the right teams to operate those systems and the right management to organize and guide the teams. We could then focus on optimizing those systems instead of endlessly 'putting out fires.'

This is game-changing! Many newer business owners try to solve every problem by focusing on HOW questions…

- How can I improve my webinar show up rate?
- How can I sell more to my existing customers?
- How can I create a recurring revenue model?

But 'crossing the threshold' also means looking at WHO questions without yourself in the chart...

- Who can get me more sales?
- Who can hire the best employees?
- Who can organize these systems for me?

Make sure you focus on creating systems that generate consistent results and then make sure you have the right people running those systems for you. This is the pathway to true freedom, power, and profit as an agency owner.

Another benefit of this kind of business-systems view is that you know when a problem emerges in the company, it's almost always a systems issue, rather than a people issue. People aren't dumb, and it's probably an unclear system that breaks, rather than the person "not getting it."

TAKEAWAY TIP: What are the systems that drive results in your business? Map them out in each department and make sure you build a team to operate and optimize the systems.

▶ **What is the greatest skill you needed to develop to be as successful as you are?**
Communication.
Outbound, over-communication.

Communication is key to every area of life and business and every time we have invested in improving our communication, our income and impact has always increased exponentially.

Think about it. Everything is communication!

SALES AND MARKETING: Communicating our value to the market in a way that drives RESULTS.

LEADERSHIP & MANAGEMENT: Communication our expectations and vision to our team in a way that drives RESULTS.

Most of our service delivery is communication too. It's helping our clients to communicate their messages better using YouTube to attract, engage and convert their dream customers online without needing paid ads.

One of the areas communication is useful in an agency is in helping build up the company culture.

"Culture eats strategy for breakfast"- Peter Drucker

It's true! If you have a brilliant strategy but a poor team you won't get as far as you will with a poor strategy but a brilliant team. The foundation of your culture is your vision and your values but the thing that builds that culture is your communication. Here are some of the things we've learned about effective communication…

Clarity is key: The first step to effective communication is knowing what IMPACT you want your communication to have. What do you want to have happen after you finish speaking? Get really clear on what impact you want so you can focus on what your message needs to be in order to get that impact. Focus on ONE goal and get super-clear about what that one goal is. Confused communication is ineffective communication

Emotion drives action: "Emotion is energy in motion." We've probably all heard that saying at some point. The thing that drives results is action and the thing that drives action is emotion. Once you know what impact you want to have you can focus on what emotion will support that impact. With our marketing we're normally trying to generate excitement, interest, curiosity, conviction etc. With our team we're normally trying to generate excitement, enthusiasm, cheerfulness, motivation etc.

Communicate about what matters and communicate often: A common stumbling block people have around communication is that they'll decide that 'now isn't the best time,' or they'll discuss easier, simpler issues and let the big stuff slide. We need to build cultures of openness and accountability in our agencies. If we let the small stuff slide it will become difficult to tackle the bigger stuff when it arises. If people aren't doing their best or are delivering sub-standard work, we need to call it out and discuss it quickly, otherwise we do a massive disservice to everyone involved. If we let it slide or brush it off, we indirectly communicate that they aren't important, that their work isn't valued. We aim to take advantage of every opportunity for personal and professional growth.

Don't be afraid to be open and vulnerable (authenticity is a super-power): There is always a massive value to showing up authentically. Don't pretend to be a superhero. Don't pretend to be invulnerable. Don't be afraid to let your unique self shine through. The more authentic you are the more it will call the people around you to also be authentic.

> "Habit 5 - Seek first to understand, then to be understood"
> - Steven Covey

Engineer outbound, over-communication with clients: Do not wait for your clients to reach out to you with questions about their project with you. They should know because you have kept them updated. This lesson came swiftly from personal experience several years ago, after committing the sin of the opposite. Fight the inner urge to feel you're being annoying or a pest by sending another message with an update. "Engineer outbound over-communication into everything"
-Alex Charfen.

▶ **What was the greatest mindset or identity shift you had to have to be as successful as you are?**

The greatest mindset shift we've made is the transition from being entrepreneurs who are waiting for every business question to get answered prior to taking action, to being entrepreneurs who knew we'd figure it out on the way, and the path would look different as we walked. That one comes with practice and everyone goes through it.

But the surprising mindset shift required for the next level is going from "person who solves everything" to "person who builds up other leaders who solve everything." That doesn't mean you don't solve any issues, but it means you change your way of thinking from being the 'primary-problem-solver' to being a 'primary-people-builder.'

In our company, we take the view that 'issues' are a good thing and a blessing in disguise because they literally point to where our attention should be and enable us to constantly grow, adapt, and improve. We have meetings every week focused on identifying and solving the issues that arise in every department. This is part of what keeps us growing as a company. If there aren't enough issues to solve… that becomes the issue!

Part of leadership is that you stop just selling your services and you start selling your vision. You create a vision that is bigger than you are. It is a vision hat is so compelling that it attracts other people who want to be part of it. You then focus on building up the people and processes that can turn that vision into a reality.

How can you accelerate that mindset shift? Start asking yourself better quality questions!

- What would I create if I knew I couldn't fail?
- What's the most amazing, epic future I can imagine creating?
- Why is this vision important to me?
- How can I spend more time being strategic and less time in the tactics?
- Would everyone know what their daily, weekly, monthly, and quarterly tasks are if we DIDN'T have meetings for 3 months? What would happen?
- Do I have a business (set of cashflowing and fulfilling systems) or am I PERSONALLY the business?
- Do I jump in to solve everything myself, or do I pause to ask, 'who's over that problem and what system is unclear?'
- Does the business know how to operate without me?
- What can I do to get a strategic edge in the marketplace?
- What are the 'ordinary things' that when done consistently will produce extraordinary outcomes?

Make sure that you plan some 'strategic thinking time' in your schedule regularly. We take "Vision Trips" to help expand what we believe is possible and once your business can run day-to-day without you, that IS your job, to be visionary and a pioneer.

Allow yourself to ask deep questions and answer them and just take the time to dream! It's easy to 'react' as a business owner, but the ability to 'respond' is the stuff of leaders. Finally, it's those that 'create' that become the legends.

Want To Know More About the YouTube Lead Machine?
Learn How To Turn YouTube Into Your Very Own Daily Organic Lead Machine: **https://vipleadmachine.com**

My Gold Nugget Takeaways

The Owners

Chapter 3
Nik Robbins

Nik Robbins is an entrepreneur who built a multi 7 figure ads agency focused on servicing doctors and has coached hundreds of aspiring agency owners through his Krusaders consulting programs.

He is on a mission to empower individuals to take control of their lives by helping them create highly profitable businesses and become the best version of themselves.

Seven years ago while having drinks on a beach for New Years with one of my best friends, I made a decision that would forever change the trajectory of my life.

I was going to leave my job in the NFL working for the Tampa Bay Buccaneers and move to Utah to start a local business marketing agency. Little did I know that decision would take me on the ride of a lifetime and change my life in ways that I could never have imagined, beginning with taking over an ENTIRE year to generate my first sale, all the way to building a consistent multiple 7 figure agency.

Since then, our agency has:

- Served over 650 medical clinics in 45+ states
- Generated over $13 million in revenue
- Helped doctors generate tens of millions in new patient revenue
- Helped our doctors heal thousands of patients
- Won multiple 2 Comma Club awards and a 2 Comma Club X award

I've been blessed to coach/work directly with over 300 agency owners and indirectly serve thousands to help them grow.

While the last seven years have been filled with immense pain, hardships, and failures, I wouldn't trade the experience for anything.

Through this journey, I've been able to:

- ✓ Find the wife of my dreams.
- ✓ Move to my dream city (Boca Raton, Florida)
- ✓ Meet most of my current best friends…
- ✓ Build a portfolio of real estate properties and investments…

And I've experienced more personal growth than I could have ever expected, which interestingly enough has been the greatest gift of all.

▶ **What was the greatest piece of advice you received from a mentor or coach that made the biggest impact in your agency journey?**

It was April 2016. I had moved to Utah thirteen months earlier to start a marketing agency with a friend, and we were sitting at zero clients. We were over $25,000 in debt and I was surviving by gambling on DraftKings/FanDuel every night.

I had tried so many methods of prospecting and I just wasn't getting any traction. One day while scrolling Facebook, I saw an ad that changed everything. It was from a guy preaching a new prospecting method that "worked every time" and the answers were sitting on a flash drive that he was selling for $9.95. The ad was from Billy Gene.

I immediately purchased the flash drive and took the $27 upsell to get digital access to the information immediately (man, he's a good marketer). And what I learned on that simple little "flash drive" was the greatest business advice I've ever received: "Use video prospecting alongside Facebook Ads to get clients."

This one piece of advice took our "agency" from zero clients and $1,000 in revenue in our first year to over $100,000 a month in recurring revenue in just ten months. And we've hit 6 figures a month every month since.

Looking back, the reason it was so powerful was not really the "tactic" of Facebook ads, it was the clarity of niching down your service and your niche.

In the agency world, we often discuss choosing your industry niche (the niche you serve, which is extremely important) but it's not as common to discuss niching down your service and what you offer to clients.

Prior to this, I was a walking "full-service digital agency" ready to offer anything from SEO to websites to email marketing to Google ads, all while not really being an expert at any of those services. And I definitely didn't know what problems my services were solving for prospects, which led to having zero clients after an entire year of trying.

Once I realized that I was ONLY going to offer Facebook Ads and we were going to utilize direct response to bring in specific customers for our specific niche, we took off. "One niche-one service-one solution" is the mentality I became obsessed with.

The key with this concept is to start with solving one very specific problem for a very specific group of prospects. To share just how deep we took this concept, here is the tagline that exponentially grew our agency:

"We help integrated medical clinics generate more patients who have osteoarthritis of the knee and need hyaluronic acid injections."

Yes, my prospecting messaging was that specific. And boy, did it work.

I discovered that not all patients are created equal in the doctor's eyes - so I honed in on the types of patients the clinics we worked with actually wanted and were the most profitable for them.

Imagine a doctor who receives 45 marketing messages a day with people saying they can bring him new patients and compare that to our message which said we could bring him the exact type of patient that he wanted. Not only does niching down your service and solution make prospecting infinitely easier... It makes sales and fulfillment much easier as well.

If you are selling the same product to the same market using the same messaging and same fulfillment processes over and over, it makes your entire business much simpler.

Simple scales - complex fails.

Be very careful of adding too much complexity to your agency—especially at the beginning—unless it's completely unnecessary. It is significantly better to become REALLY good at solving one problem for your client (ideally one that makes them a lot of money) than it is to be mediocre at many different things.

▶ **What would you say was the biggest contributing factor to your success?**

I'll never forget the feeling of waking up on the cold concrete floor in a Sacramento County jail cell in April of 2010. The memories of the night before were blurry. My head throbbed with pain, and I was filled with a sense of dread and regret that I'll remember forever.

I had been arrested for a DUI. It was the 3rd time in 18 months I had been arrested for alcohol related issues and it was an enormous slap in the face. I had put others' lives in jeopardy, I had put my own life in jeopardy, and I had let my parents down. I was so ashamed of myself.

They say that "the worst times of your life are often the best things that ever happen to you" and that turned out to be the case for me.

About a week after receiving the DUI, I was talking to one of my fraternity brothers about the experience and he gave me one of the ultimate blessings of my life. He handed me a book called *A New Earth* by Eckhart Tolle. I finished the entire thing in three days, and the book completely changed the way I view reality and life.

Around that same time, my dad mailed me the book *Awaken the Giant Within* by Tony Robbins.

After reading these books, something shifted inside of me, and I became obsessed with personal development. I came to the realization that if I continued to feed my brain with new information (from self-improvement to skill development), it would change my thoughts which would change my behavior which would change my life.

Because of that realization, I've spent over $500,000 in the past five years trying to grow my mindset and my skills. From books to masterminds to personal development seminars and courses, this money has been the best money I have ever spent, and those investments have changed the trajectory of my life.

Those investments in my mindset and my skills took me from being a guy who was arrested 3 times in 18 months to an entrepreneur who has done over $15,000,000 in sales and coached hundreds of other entrepreneurs

Without a doubt, the biggest contributing factor to my success has been my obsession with personal development and growth.

Being an entrepreneur is tough and anyone who tells you otherwise is probably trying to sell you something. When you're building a business, you do a lot of things for the first time, and it can be scary. You're putting yourself outside your comfort zone. You're making mistakes. You're doing things you've never done before. And it can be overwhelming.

Entrepreneurship can be summed up in essentially one word: Problems. And the way you view problems is going to determine your success or failure.

- How do you react when you are told no over and over again?
- When you barely have enough money to make ends meet?
- When you have to struggle to hit payroll?
- When a client tells you that "you suck" and fires you?
- When an employee or customer steals your material?
- When you have to miss time with friends/family in order to work?

Without personal development, dealing with these thoughts and problems can feel overwhelming and almost impossible.

When you focus on building your mind, you can approach problems with a totally different mindset. To quote the legendary Captain Jack Sparrow:

"The problem is not the problem. The problem is the attitude you have about the problem."

Because of this, whenever I am working with newer entrepreneurs, I always tell them "I can teach you all of the tactics in the world but unless you master your psychology, you will struggle to take action on the tactics and struggle to survive the warzone that is being an entrepreneur."

The mind is almost always our biggest enemy and the thing stopping us from getting the results we want in life. You must be able win the war with your mind before you can win the war on the entrepreneurial battleground.

▶ **What is the greatest skill you needed to develop to be as successful as you are?**

I have a two-part answer to this question as I believe that in order to win at the game of entrepreneurship you must master two things:

1. Sales
2. Skillset-acquisition

▶ **PART 1:**

As a fresh account executive, I was sitting across the desk from my mentor, Deno, who was the Director of Sales at the Tampa Bay Buccaneers. Deno made a statement that forever changed my life.

"Great salespeople do not need to be aggressive, they need to be assertive. You just happen to see many aggressive sales people at the top of the leaderboard because they are automatically assertive due to their aggressive approach."

I had just told him that I was uncertain in my ability to sell because at that point, I believed that all great salespeople were aggressive, and that wasn't me. His response instilled a level of certainty in me that I wouldn't have to change my personality to win at sales.

After that conversation, I shot straight to the top of the sales leaderboard at the Buccaneers and then went on to close over $15,000,000 in sales for my own companies.

Since then, I've come to realize that sales are the lifeblood of business. Without sales, you don't have a business. Without sales, you can't pay your employees and invest in your company. Without sales, you can't get your products into the hands of people who need them.

Selling has been by far the most valuable skill set I have developed over the years and one I continue to sharpen to this day. Many people often have a negative connotation around sales, and I understand why. There are people out there who use persuasion and influence to do unethical things.

But with that said, if you have a product or a service that can transform an individual or business's life, the only way to get them to experience the transformation is by being able to sell it to them.

After working directly with hundreds of agency owners, I can say with 100% certainty that the number one factor in how quickly they will see success is their ability to sell.

The agency owners who come from a sales background almost always outperform those who don't in the early stages of building their agency. (This does not mean that if you don't have a sales background you can't succeed). Becoming good at sales is not just about business either; your ability to persuade your friends/partner/kids will have a dramatic impact on your quality of life.

If you are reading this with a knot in your stomach and thinking something along the lines of "I am just not good at sales," or "Sales people are unethical," understand that this is a belief system you have adopted and that does not need to be true.

The fact is, we are all selling all day everyday (including selling ourselves on concepts like "I am not good at sales.") We might as well become good at it!

▶ PART 2:

If I had to choose any individual specific skill that has had the biggest impact on my career it would be sales without question. I believe everyone should actually master the skill of being able to acquire more skills. And to take that to the next level, they should learn to be intentional about what complimentary skills they stack together to forge themselves into a true weapon.

Many people are under this illusion that we "learn business" but that is not the case. "Business" is not a skill. It is made up of a many different underlying components such as:

- Sales
- Marketing
- Product Development
- Finance
- ETC

Each of these is a skill set we can acquire. The order in which they are learned is based upon the individual, and there is no "right" or "wrong" path. My recommendation to you is that you become deliberate about which ones you acquire and the order in which you acquire them.

Skills can be stacked together in a way that leads to exponential returns. The more deliberate you are with this process, the bigger the returns.

Let me give you an example of skill stacking:

- The first skill I learned was sales (started getting results)
- Then I learned marketing and the ability to run paid traffic to set my own inbound appointments (exponential increase in results)
- Then I learned how to build products on my own that I could sell (exponential increase in results)

- Then I learned how to systemize my sales process so that anyone could duplicate my results (exponential increase in results)

- Then I learned how to hire, recruit, and train sales closers to use my systems and sell my products (exponential increase in results)

- And the next skillset I am acquiring is investing and wealth multiplication. (Which will lead to exponential increase in results)

With every new skill added, I massively increased my leverage which in turn increased my results in business. You can do this in any domain you choose. Let's do an example with copywriting:

- First you learn how to write good copy to sell other people's products

- Then you learn how to build funnels

- Then you learn how to run paid traffic

- Then you learn how to build your own products

- Then you learn how to hire and train copywriters to write on your behalf

With every new skill added, your potential increases dramatically.

I recommend you start to be deliberate about your skill-set acquisition and you'll start to see compounding results.

▶ **What was the greatest mindset or identity shift you had to have to be as successful as you are?**

In the following, I will share both a mindset shift and an identity shift.

MINDSET SHIFT:

At 27 years old I was driving home one freezing cold snowy day in the winter of 2015 living in Utah after another day of being told "no" to trying to sell my agency services. Over the previous 8 months, I had been feeling lost, confused, and unsure how to succeed in business and in life.

My initial confidence in building an agency had begun to suffer dramatically. I was listening to a motivational speech by Les Brown and he spoke a quote that has become my number one operating system towards life:

"People are always blaming their circumstances for what they are. I don't believe in circumstances. The people who get on in this world are the people who get up and look for the circumstances they want... and if they can't find them, they MAKE them." - George Bernard Shaw

And that was the moment that I fully took responsibility for my life. I accepted that everything that happens in life (both good and bad) is MY fault. I blame nobody else but myself for my circumstances. The internal power that arises from this belief system is indescribable.

Of course, there are things outside our control, and there might be things that are actually holding you back, but what useful purpose does blaming someone else or something else have for us?

There have been countless times over the years where I've wanted to blame Zuckerberg for recklessly shutting down an ad account, clients that suck the life out of me, or countless other bad things that have happened...

But I always remind myself that I am in control of my circumstances. Blaming others will do nothing to help me reach a solution to the problems in front of me.

IDENTITY SHIFT:

"You can't outperform your self-image" - Inky Johnson.

Identity or self-image is a difficult concept to articulate but it's an important thing to be aware of as you will behave in accordance to how you view yourself.

In late 2017 at a private mastermind in Dallas I spoke with a 21-year-old who told me he was taking home $100,000 a month income making YouTube videos. I remember thinking, "This is just a normal dude doing normal things. There was nothing overtly special about him or his videos."

I say this not to demean this individual—in fact quite the opposite—I was unbelievably impressed and for the first time it made me truly expand my belief in what was possible. It created within me an instant shift in my identity and allowed me to see a much larger vision for myself.

This shift in identity led to me taking massive action on new initiatives that I never would have undertaken had I not had this conversation.

Over the years I have spent a lot of time thinking about identities and how to shift them, and after thinking through the biggest identity shifts that happened in my life and HOW they happened, I realized that there are three things that typically take place whenever I upgrade my identity.

- I must first have a vision for who I want to become
- I immerse myself with people who are getting the result I am looking to obtain
- 30 Day Massive intense action

Why do these 3 things work so well in unison? First, we are able to visualize and see who we want to become, which is the critical first step in creating the highest versions of ourselves.

Then we are able to have our own internal beliefs broken around what is possible by fully immersing ourselves within a community or mastermind group of individuals who are already getting the result we want.

Then we are able to start seeing quick wins and results utilizing our 30-day massive action plan which leads to us using evidence that reinforces our visualization. All of this leads to a circular effect that will shift your identity over time.

▶ **In Summary:**

If you've made it this far, I know you are willing to put in the work to make it in the agency game.

Here are a couple of final thoughts:

- Be wary of shiny object syndrome and stay focused on building your agency
- Remove negative influences from your life (this especially includes family/friends)
- Join communities focused on building agencies
- Stay the course. Entrepreneurship is a battle of perseverance

- Never give up
- HAVE FUN!

I wish you the best of luck on your journey and would love to connect on social media!

If you would like to learn more about building your business, follow Nik's YouTube Channel:
https://www.youtube.com/channel/UCgDxTDuo-qHCD9VeUDKKBCA

My Gold Nugget Takeaways

The Owners

Chapter 4
Andrew Stickel

Andrew Stickel helps lawyers be more productive and happier, both personally and professionally. He formed a marketing agency called Social Firestarter in 2012 to help lawyers grow their law firms, get more clients, and optimize their time to be successful while still having a life outside of work. In 2022, Social Firestarter merged with SMB Team to become the fastest-growing non-software company in the legal industry. Through his free online training, done-for-you services, and coaching program, Andrew has helped tens of thousands of lawyers worldwide.

Andrew enjoys spending time with his wife and three kids and wants to give the lawyers he works with the time and comfort to do the same themselves.

Lessons I Learned Growing a $20 Million/Year Agency

In August of 2012, my first child was born. So naturally, this was not the ideal time to launch a brand-new business, let alone a marketing agency. I set up my laptop at my kitchen table and got to work without a clue of who I was going to do marketing for, how I would get clients, or even what I would do once I got them.

Fast forward ten years, and that company has more than 50 employees and generates more than $20 million per year in revenue.

Along the way, I've learned many lessons, most of which, had I known them sooner, would have rapidly increased my success rate and made me much more money. Growing a marketing agency is pretty easy if you embrace the following lessons which took me ten years to learn.

▶ **What was the greatest piece of advice you received from a mentor or coach that made the biggest impact in your agency journey?**

Lesson 1: The Riches Are in the Niches

Blah blah blah, we've all heard "niche down" before, but that doesn't make it any less accurate. Thankfully, I didn't learn this lesson the hard way. Instead, I got lucky and fell into an incredible niche: attorneys.

Before we started the agency, my partner (now retired) was the national sales director at one of the largest marketing agencies in the world for lawyers. She was leaving that position because she finally realized that, although she was selling packages to lawyers for tens of thousands of dollars, the agency was doing next to nothing for their clients. She had a moral epiphany and wanted to do something meaningful.

When we started our agency, we didn't intend to focus on lawyers. We intended to start a social media agency that did marketing for everyone. However, we needed some seed money, and she knew some lawyers who wanted help with their social media. She made a few calls, and suddenly we had some money in the bank. Initially, we started with two lawyers, then four lawyers, then eight, then 16, and before we knew it, we became a "lawyer marketing agency" almost by accident.

It turns out we accidentally picked a fantastic niche for a few reasons:

1. The legal industry doesn't follow GDP. This means that it isn't affected by recession or a pandemic. In 2020, we didn't lose a single client due to Covid-19. 2020 was a record year for us (2021 was even better than 2021, and 2022 has been better than 2021). When picking a niche, find a niche that doesn't follow GDP. Niches like legal, medical, and HVAC are great examples of this. If your air conditioner goes out in the middle of summer, Covid or not, most people are getting it fixed.

2. Lawyers have a high transaction value. We've helped personal injury lawyer clients get cases that have resulted in $25 million settlements. At that rate, one case has paid for our services for the rest of their career. Even practice areas with lower average

transaction values (for the legal industry) like estate planning, family law, or criminal defense command several thousand dollars per client. This makes it very easy for the clients to break even and profit from your services. Compare this to a pizza shop. How many slices of pizza must they sell just to pay your retainer? Focus on businesses that can get an ROI from your service as quickly as possible.

In real estate, profit is made when you buy, not sell. The same goes for a marketing agency. The entire foundation of your business depends on your decision regarding the markets you choose to serve. Do yourself a massive favor and pick an industry that will provide security for decades.

▶ **What would you say was the biggest contributing factor to your success?**

Lesson 2: Take Ownership in Their Result

If holes dug themselves, no one would ever buy a shovel. One lesson that took me entirely too long to learn is a simple one: the ONLY reason clients hire an agency is that they are looking for a result. In my legal marketing agency, that result is getting more clients for their law firms.

So, it stands to reason that clients will be happy if we focus on that single result. Initially, I made the mistake of focusing on things that didn't matter—vanity metrics that made people feel good but ended up with disgruntled clients who fired us.

For example, a big part of our agency is building websites and performing search engine optimization, also known as SEO. Every month we would report where they ranked for particular keywords, how many phone calls they got and how much website traffic they received.

These were indicators that something was happening, but they don't tell the whole story about whether or not the client was happy. For example, we once got a client 300 phone calls in a single month. Indeed, that client was thrilled, right? Wrong. He failed to turn a single phone call into a case. Even worse, he blamed us, and we were on the brink of getting fired!

After some investigating, we found many of the phone calls went unanswered because he didn't have anyone to answer the calls. The ones he talked to failed to turn into clients because he was terrible at sales.

It would have been easy to blame the client, but that would have been a significant misstep and cost us lots of money. After all, if we got fired every time clients didn't do their part, we'd constantly be replacing clients!

So instead, we asked ourselves a question: how can we take as much responsibility as possible for the end result, even if it is something they are responsible for as business owners?

This question fundamentally changed my marketing agency forever. For one, we realized that lawyers couldn't get clients if no one answers the phone when a lead calls. Instead of complaining, we worked out a deal with an answering service. Now, we provide a free answering service for all our clients, and unanswered calls are a thing of the past.

But what happens when a lawyer gets on the phone with a lead but doesn't know how to close the deal? Well, that too is a thing of the past, because we provide all of our clients with comprehensive sales training.

What about when the lawyer does a great job at sales, and the prospect wants to buy, but doesn't have the money? Well, they're in luck because we hook them up with a funding company that will provide personal loans to their clients so they can get paid.

Most marketing agencies lose clients left and right, but not us. Our average client sticks with us for nearly four years. The average net promoter score of a marketing agency is zero, and ours is consistently in the 80s for one reason: we understand the result that our clients care about, and we structure our offer to include everything that will give them the best chance of achieving the result.

This brings me to my next lesson...

What is the greatest skill you needed to develop to be as successful as you are?

Lesson 3: Make an Incredible Offer They Can't Get Anywhere Else

When you take ownership of the result, you start to find solutions that will deliver the results they are looking for. These solutions not only deliver better results but also handle objections and allow you to create an offer that your clients can't get anywhere else, making it impossible for them to price shop.

For example, as an SEO agency, one of the issues we always deal with is the objection that "SEO takes too long." It's true. It does take a long time to rank a lawyer on the first page of Google, especially in a competitive niche. Our solution: we'll run your Google and Facebook ads campaigns for free so you can get the phone ringing immediately. This handles the time delay objection while simultaneously creating a better offer and delivering the result they are looking for: leads and clients.

Another problem we had was that most of our clients didn't get Google reviews regularly. Google reviews are essential for both ranking in Google and providing social proof. Our solution was to create software that allows them to get Google reviews on autopilot in a way that increases their Google rankings in the process.

For years we complained that our clients didn't get enough reviews, and as a result, we couldn't deliver their results. As soon as we changed our complaint to the question, "How can we help them get reviews?" we ended up with a solution. When a law firm hires us, we provide proprietary software that automatically gets them more reviews, allowing them to rank higher in Google and get more phone calls and clients, which is the result they're looking for. Additionally, the solution becomes part of the offer: when they hire us, they get this fantastic software that they can't get anywhere else.

Another example of this is a website chat box. We noticed that most people visit websites without contacting our clients for a consultation. We also noticed that some of our clients had third-party chat services, and many of them produced additional leads. Knowing that the end result is clients for our clients, and clients come from leads, we worked out a deal with a chat box provider to provide a free website chat box for all our clients, staffed by a real person 24/7. Now, our clients have another way to get leads from their website, making it more likely they'll achieve the result they want: clients.

Once our clients started growing, we identified another problem: they didn't have the staff to handle the new cases. Most of our clients didn't even know how to run a business—they were great lawyers, not business owners. They didn't know anything about hiring, creating standard operating procedures (SOPs), holding employees accountable using key performance indicators (KPIs), creating annual and quarterly goals, and so much more. This hindered their ability to grow and make money, which hindered our ability to grow and make money because as clients got too many cases, they wanted to dial back services.

This resulted in our business's coaching division, where we teach lawyers how to run their law firm like a business. We also launched The Legal Marketing Academy, which teaches them everything they need to know about marketing their law firm (above and beyond what we do for them). We also teach them how to get the most out of our marketing services, which ensures that we get better results.

Our offer is constantly evolving and will continue to evolve as we further identify the needs of our clients, but consider how it started and where it currently stands:

Original offer ($2,497/Month): Website, SEO, Monthly Blogging

Current offer ($6,497/Month): Website, SEO, Monthly Blogging, Social Media Management, Facebook/Google Ads, 24/7 Answering Service, Unlimited Website Chats, Review Software, SMB Coaching Program, Legal Marketing Academy Coaching Program, Sales Training, Client Funding

As we added services, we also increased our prices. This is partly due to increased expenses, but our profit also increased. Even better, we lose fewer clients now, even though the price is nearly triple what we used to charge. They are getting an ROI because we're arming them with all the tools necessary to achieve their desired result: getting more clients so they can grow their business.

▶ **What was the greatest mindset or identity shift you had to have to be as successful as you are?**

Lesson 4: The Sales Process Doesn't Begin on The Sales Call

I was on stage in a room with about 50 lawyers in 2019. Before this event, I had never met any of the lawyers in the room. "By a show of hands, how many people in this room have never met me before today, yet you feel like you've known me for years." I looked around the room as every single hand went up in unison.

This wasn't surprising; it was merely a confirmation of what I already knew. The more goodwill you put into the marketplace, the more people will know, like, and trust you, and THAT has been my secret to growing an agency fast.

Since 2018, I have been creating helpful videos for lawyers. As of this writing, I have more than 1,300 actionable YouTube videos that teach lawyers how to grow. I email them daily tips and tricks about how to get clients. I run video view ads on Facebook and Instagram with no CTA–only marketing tips for lawyers. I've written two books. I share every single tip, trick, hack, secret, and strategy I know publicly and for free.

And the result? I've become a household name as someone lawyers can trust to help them learn how to get more clients. And when they realize they don't have time to do this stuff themselves, or they simply don't want to, who do you think they call? (Hint: Me).

One thing I was initially worried about, and a question I always hear is, "If you tell them exactly how to market their law firms, won't they just do it themselves?" A few will take your advice and do it themselves, but most won't. And the ones who do it themselves were never going to hire you in the first place, so who cares? Just put the content out there you'll be shocked at the results.

You may also think, "But Andy, you have 1,300 videos, a Facebook group full of potential clients, an email list, etc." That's true, but I started with no video, no email list, and nothing else to fall back on.

In 2017, I bought a Canon DSLR camera with the specific intention of filming videos. That camera sat on my desk for six months, collecting dust before I filmed my first (terrible) video. No one knew who I was, and no one cared. But I kept going. I kept filming videos and creating value. As I filmed, I progressively improved each time and gained momentum. It took me four months of filming multiple videos every day to get my first lead (not client...lead).

The best part about this strategy is that it's just hard enough to make your competition quit. It isn't that filming videos is hard–that gets pretty easy. The hardest part is sticking with it, and 99% of your competition will quit at the first sign of difficulty. The secret to winning this game is understanding that if you just keep going, eventually, you'll end up winning.

Rand Fishkin calls this "The Gap of Disappointment," and I can attest that it is your absolute best friend.

Here's how the Gap of Disappointment works. When you first create content, you are in the Honeymoon phase. You will have lots of ideas and topics to discuss, so creating a few videos is easy. On top of that, because it's new and people haven't seen you creating content, you will get lots of comments, shares, and likes on your videos. This gives you an excellent ROI (not a monetary ROI, but an emotional ROI in the form of dopamine hits).

But then, "The Slog" kicks in. Creating content becomes more challenging because you have to think of new topics continually, life gets in the way, and it becomes less of a priority. Combine that with the fact that you're not getting those dopamine hits because it's not new anymore, and people are now accustomed to you creating content.

This is where most people quit. However, the ones who keep going and refuse to quit are the ones that benefit on the other side of the gap of disappointment, also known as "Equilibrium." This is where ROI skyrockets and effort plummets.

The problem is that most people don't know this stage exists and quit before they get there.

Today, I get hundreds of leads without much effort, and that will happen to you if you just don't quit. Want the secret to winning? Don't quit.

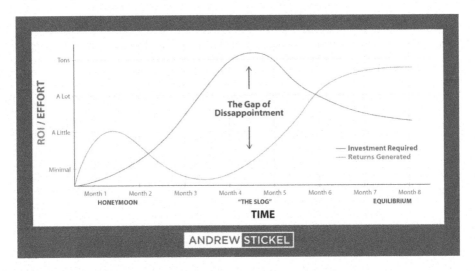

If you want to create content but are unsure where to start, try using this simple hack I've been using for years to create content. This is the same hack I share with my clients when I teach them to film videos:

3. Make a list of every single problem your ideal clients have.

4. Write down a simple solution to each problem.

5. Think of a story or parable than can be used to teach them the solution to each problem.

I usually start with a chart that looks like this:

Problem	Solution	Story

For example, one problem my clients have is getting Google reviews. They know they need more reviews but struggle to get their clients to leave them. Often, they ask their clients to leave a review, and the client agrees but never actually posts the review.

The solution to the elusive Google review is to provide a reason why you need the Google review because people are more likely to comply with a request if they have a reason.

The story I tell for this particular problem involves a Harvard social psychologist named Ellen Langer:

Langer demonstrated a valuable principle of human behavior. She found that if we ask someone to do us a favor, we'll have more people comply with our request if we give a reason. People are more likely to do what you want if provided a reason for the request. Langer experimented involving a copy machine. She waited for a line to form and then attempted to skip ahead to the front of the line.

First, she gave a strong excuse: "Excuse me, I have five pages. May I use the copy machine because I'm in a rush?" Asking to skip the line in this manner resulted in a success rate of 94%.

Next, she asked again but provided no reason: "Excuse me, I have five pages. May I use the copy machine?" This time, she was only successful 60% of the time.

Finally, she gave another reason, but it was pretty weak this time: "Excuse me, I have five pages. May I use the copy machine because I have to make some copies?" Again, the success rate increased to 93%, even though the reason was weak (EVERYONE was there to make copies).

Langer successfully demonstrated the power of the word "because." When you give people a reason, no matter how small, they are more likely to comply with your request.

So, if you want more people to leave you a review for your law firm, you must give them a reason why you need the review. Don't just ask, "Will you please leave us a review?"

Instead, try, "Picking an attorney can be one of the most difficult and important decisions someone makes, but often, people don't know who to pick. Reviews from clients like you help more people make potentially one of the most important decisions of their lives."

So, in this instance, my chart would look like this:

Problem	Solution	Story
CLIENTS WON'T LEAVE REVIEWS	GIVE THEM A REASON	XEROX MACHINE STORY

Finally, you may wonder where I get my content; the answer is everywhere! This particular example I pulled from the book *Persuasion* by Robert Cialdini. However, I pull stories from my everyday life, lessons learned from playing with my kids, client examples, books I read, movies, Tik Tok videos, and anywhere else. The secret is to look at your life experiences and ask yourself what lessons they can help teach your clients. Always be looking for stories you can use to create content.

If you want to see how I use stories to solve problems on a grander scale, check out my book *5-Star Attorney* (available on Amazon), which teaches lawyers how to get reviews and use reviews to make money. Although you may not be an attorney, it is worth reading to witness how I weave stories throughout the book to illustrate my lessons.

If you create content and continue to create content regularly, people will begin to binge-watch your content and, as strange as this sounds, will look at you as a celebrity. They'll begin to know, like, and trust you, and people hire people they know, like, and trust. If I had to guess, I'd estimate that this process alone is responsible for 80% of the rapid growth of my business.

▶ A Few More Short Lessons

Over the last ten years, I've learned countless lessons as I've grown as both a marketing agency owner and an entrepreneur—too many to catalog in this short chapter.

However, the four lessons I've shared with you are the ones that, when implemented, will move the needle for you and your agency the fastest.

Because I'm running short on the remaining word count, in this final section, I've decided to go into a few more short lessons, in no particular order, that have also proven pivotal to our success.

▶ Responsiveness and Client Check-Ins

We send net promoter score (NPS) surveys to our clients each month to get a pulse on how things are going. This is vitally important because it allows us to identify a potentially unhappy clients before they decide to cancel with us. If we know they're unhappy, we can often save them. One comment we get over and over is about the responsiveness of our team. Believe it or not, clients notice how quickly you respond to their emails, phone calls, and messages, which is often reflected in their NPS scores. One of the easiest ways to keep clients happy: respond quickly.

Another hack we've used for years is the client check-in. When I first started the agency, I met with every single client for about an hour once per month. I did this for about five years, and we didn't lose a single client during this time. Unfortunately, as we scale past 350 clients, I can't meet with clients anymore. However, we now have a team of client experience representatives who meet with clients to check in, make sure they are happy, and advocate on their behalf if they aren't. The squeaky wheel gets the grease, but most clients won't be squeaky wheels; they'll just cancel their services. Monthly check-ins allow us to keep our clients happy by addressing issues before they become severe enough for the client to cancel.

▶ The Only Way to Scale is Client Retention

This goes without saying, but you can't grow your business if you constantly lose clients. A lot of the time, marketing agencies focus too much on getting new clients and not enough on keeping the clients they have. The most challenging part of the entire relationship with a client is the first six months. After the first six months, we've typically delivered enough of a result for them to trust us so we can continue to help them grow. When you lose clients, you're constantly repeating the most challenging part over and over again.

We found that if you focus on keeping the clients happy and delivering results, then scaling your agency is so much easier for a few reasons:

- ◆ First, because you're focusing on getting results for clients, you figure out how to get results. When clients get results, clients tend to stick around, so you don't lose revenue.

- Second, when clients get results, clients give you testimonials, which you can use as social proof to get more clients.

- Third, when clients get results, they're happy to refer their friends, allowing you to get even more clients.

Once you focus on client retention, your business will scale exponentially faster.

Live Events = Massive Growth

I was debating even including live events on this list because it would take an entire book to give that strategy the justice it deserves. One of the easiest and most effective ways to add lots of clients in a short period of time is hosting live events. For example, we host at least one virtual sales event per quarter, and each event typically generates at least $1 million in annual revenue for the business.

One mistake often made during live events is failing to plan the content properly. The key to planning your event content is that every piece of content should be planned to get you closer to the sale. If the content doesn't teach a belief or a concept that will ultimately get them closer to buying your offer, it doesn't belong in the event. People often create content just for the sake of creating content; all this does is kill your sales.

When we plan our events, we first plan the offer. Then, we ask ourselves, "What MUST our clients believe for them to buy our offer?" Once we have that answer, we work backward and plan the content accordingly. This method hasn't failed us yet.

▶ Conclusion

Perhaps the biggest lesson I've learned in life came from Zig Ziglar when he said, "You can have everything in life you want if you will just help other people get what they want." This lesson is true in life, and it's true when running a marketing agency.

If you understand what your clients want and help them get it, you will be rewarded with an agency with massive growth. Believe it or not, the more my agency has grown, the easier my life has become. When we started, I was the one building the websites, writing the content, doing sales, and everything else. Now, we have teams for virtually every aspect of the company.

My business allows my family and me to live a life that others only dream of. I have a million-dollar home, a million-dollar vacation home; my family takes amazing vacations whenever and wherever we want, and I only work four days a week. I'm not telling you this to brag. I'm telling you this because I want to emphasize a point: none of this would be possible had I ignored the lessons I shared in this chapter. These lessons made me a multi-millionaire, and they can make you one if you let them. My ONLY regret is that I didn't implement them faster!

https://www.facebook.com/andrew.stickel.52

My Gold Nugget Takeaways

The Owners

Chapter 5
Jason Feltman

It seems like it was a long time ago, in a galaxy far, far away when we clicked "Purchase" on the ClickFunnels checkout page. Little did we know that with that click of a button, we'd become members of a very powerful collective of top performing business minds from all over the world. We knew nothing of funnels, of funnel hacking, nothing about potato guns, and had no sense for the quantum leaps that were to take place over the next few years. We are Jason Feltman and Craig Pretzinger, a couple of insurance agency owners that now serve other insurance agency owners in converting internet leads to clients. We're honored that Stephanie asked us to share our story, and are excited at the thought of our efforts, down on paper, inspiring other entrepreneurs to take their plunge into the unknown and put their own mark on the world.

The Insurance Dudes and TeleDudes TeleFunnels

▶ **What was the greatest piece of advice you received from a mentor or coach that made the biggest impact in your agency journey?**

There have been so many great pieces of advice that have made a massive impact on our business. Trying to nail down the number one best piece of advice was incredibly difficult. If you've been a part of this community for a while, there's no shortage of fantastic information that can deeply affect the impact of your business—in fact, there's so much, it's easy to go nuts wanting to do all of it! I think back to when we started all of this, one of the best pieces of advice was creating an "irresistible offer." This was a bit of a hang-up for us for a while trying to figure out exactly what would make the irresistible offer for our business. Creating an irresistible offer is much easier said than done at the beginning.

The service we provide can be viewed as a commodity, and it was for us at first. Have you ever felt that people are not going to pay a price for your service unless you lower it? We really struggled with this when we started our business. We didn't have an offer, nor were we sharing it as a "new opportunity." At the time, it was just a service, and so, the conversation typically landed on how we price the service. My business partner, Craig, wanted to charge a lot for the service and we constantly debated back-and-forth; I wanted to charge less and he wanted to charge more. Those endless discussions are really what got the ball rolling with our offer.

Dan Kennedy says, "There is no advantage in being the second lowest price leader in town, but there is a huge strategic advantage to being the most expensive." Really wrapping my head around that is really what helped me to understand that it wasn't about being price competitive, it was about being "offer-extraordinary." The question then became: "If we do charge this high price, what else could we include to make that price a great value?" If we could add-in so much value, that insane value combined with the high price actually makes the price incredibly low!

When we looked around at many offers, a lot of agencies and products include a bunch of stuff in their offer, so we thought that the best plan of action was to just offer a lot of stuff. Quickly, we learned that that is not the case. Sometimes more stuff can make the offer seem complicated and overwhelming. As we offered our service and started including more in our offer, we realized that it really came down to their *results*. What could we include with our service that would help them grow and get them the best results possible. There are a lot of agencies and services with similar offerings, but creating your own irresistible offer can really help you stand out from anyone in your industry. As you build that offer and really figure out the problems that you're solving for your clients and include those specific solutions, you will begin to specialize and differentiate yourself from the competition.

You might be thinking there are a ton of agencies out there, and the competition is incredibly tough. The irresistible offer really creates the blue ocean for your business. If you're not familiar with red ocean/blue ocean, it's a concept where the red ocean represents a market full of competitors in which most of those competitors get beat up, making it incredibly difficult to sell your product – oftentimes it becomes a price war, a race to the bottom, where no one wins.

Blue ocean is where you create your own category where there are no competitors, so beating the competition becomes irrelevant because there isn't any! The more you talk to your clients and really get to know what they like, what they hate, their biggest fears, and what success means to them, the easier it becomes to build out your offer. Figuring out what your ideal client wants is the key to creating your *blue ocean*. If you find out their biggest concerns, and then solve them, you create long-time clients.

One of the breakthroughs that we had with our agency was even if we put leads on the phone right in front of our clients, their salespeople were unable to close those leads. We knew what our most successful clients were doing so we decided to put together a framework of what to do when they received the lead. We started by putting together a script that had the key elements of what their salespeople were saying to increase the conversion rate. Then we added a weekly coaching element for their sales agents to help get them used to the script in action. Helping them with their agents' talk paths and the ongoing coaching created a massive impact in their business. We started to get incredible feedback on the coaching, with some agents going as far as saying we made such a difference in business and life.

You might find your irresistible offer the same way we did. Find your ideal client and learn the journey of the lead in their business. Find out who receives the lead and what systems and processes they have to take that lead and make them a client. Ask a ton of questions, such as:

- What does their team do?
- What do they say?
- How can you support them even after you generate leads for them?
- Is there some way you can help them close the lead?
- Are there tools that you could provide?

The more questions like these that you ask, the more answers you will find. This is something I believe should be ongoing. And don't stop asking! Tony Robbins said, "The power of our questions unlocks the quality of their responses–it shifts their focus to what's really most important."

The additional benefits of the offer have dramatically changed our retention. The better our offer has become, the longer our clients stay with us even if they are struggling to get the results they need. Why? Because we've shifted their focus to what's most important by asking the right questions. Some join the program for one reason, but they get added benefits in other areas of their business that creates new reasons for them to stay. There is never just one reason why they are not getting great results, it's usually a combination of things that end up with less than satisfying results. Finding out the reasons they are struggling and including solutions in your offer can make a huge impact.

In short, we encourage you to shoot for the stars; understand that most people never even take the first few steps due to fear of failure. As you obtain better and get better results for your clients with your offer, charge more. Don't ever let limiting beliefs hold you back from creating the cash flow in your business that will allow you to grow. This is a topic of conversation among people in the Inner Circle all the time. We hear so many incredible business owners present to the group and a constant piece of advice we hear is to increase price. Everybody seems to struggle with this. I continue to struggle with this. There is always someone willing to pay more if the offer is irresistible.

▶ **What would you say was the biggest contributing factor to your success?**

The one thing that made the biggest contribution to our success was something that certainly did not feel like it would lead anywhere at the time. When we first started, we actually didn't have a product, a service, or offer. We didn't even really know what we wanted to do.

We were a couple of insurance agents that loved to talk about all the ideas that we had for agencies. We were both starting podcasts right around the same time and had no clear direction for them, aside from that these podcasts would be insurance podcasts. I remember there wasn't really a theme for either one of ours, and on one of our calls, Craig asked, "Why we don't just do them together, I mean, we're talking all the time anyways...why don't we just combine podcasts and interview insurance agents and find out what the top agents in our industry are doing." That is how the podcast began.

In the beginning, we were just finding our way and didn't really have a structure. Those first six months were tough for us, because there were no listeners. I remember when we had three, then five, then seven, and thinking, "This is going to take forever!" Like anything else, the longer you do something, the more gains you make. Once we were six months to a year into it, we really started getting some traction and hitting some exponential growth. I think that's something that people don't realize, is that it's not a linear path. There becomes a point where after a certain amount of consistency and persistence, all of the work compounds and the reach starts multiplying. Little did we know that that podcast would be the biggest contribution to our success later on in our career.

The podcast not only contributed to the growth but became the source of inspiration for our service. We were having a blast making the podcast, but we still didn't have a business even a year and a half into it. I remember being pretty frustrated as we were trying to figure out how to serve our audience. What I didn't realize at the time, as we were learning so much from all of the people that we were interviewing, was that we were actually implementing it into our own insurance businesses.

One of those processes that we learned from the podcast became something that other agents really wanted to install in their agencies as well. Craig signed up a few people to do it by himself and asked if I wanted to be a part of it. That's when we realized that we could use the podcast and our client base and connect them with the service.

Another huge benefit of the podcast was the connections we were making. Our goal was to serve insurance agents. We got a lot of really large agency owners on the podcast and were able to pick their brains. We were also able to get incredible industry leaders outside of Insurance like Garrett White, Trey Lewelin and Robin Sharma (to name a few) on the podcast as well. These guys, especially Garrett White, would have been impossible to interview if we didn't have a podcast. It really began to create a place of networking that we never imagined possible prior to launching.

I know what you might be thinking: "What do I talk about? How do I get people on the podcast? How do I get listeners?" Those are all valid questions, but in reality, who cares! If you listen to the first episodes of our podcast, it's really cringeworthy, as we were all over the place and it was incredibly awkward. We were insurance agents that already talked to people all day long on the phone and had agencies with employees. You would think that we wouldn't be nervous to jump on a zoom call with somebody else, but like most people we were very nervous.

We also didn't have a framework for the interviews, and we'd just jump on without doing much research or any game plan. We just hopped on a call and started talking–that's it! All you have to do is just that! Let's say you do ten episodes and completely want to change everything–which is a huge possibility–then that's what you do. You can always delete the episodes, but getting started is the most important thing; it will lead to the answers of all the questions you have prior to starting.

As we kept recording episode after episode, we realized there were specific questions that really unlocked great answers, so we began to write them down. We began creating our own framework and then realized it is not about us, it is about the audience that we're serving. We asked the few listeners we had what questions they thought would be the best to ask and then included those in our new interviewing framework. We found that asking the audience what questions they want answered is a great way to go about it.

But how can you ask an audience that you don't have when you get started? Great question! There is no shortage of Facebook groups, podcasts or any other social media that has your audience in it. With any of those sources, especially Facebook groups, join them and read the comments. The comments are where all the gold is! This will help you design your podcast framework even before you get started. Don't let the research slow you down and keep you from getting started. It is easy to use "one more hour/day/week of research" as an excuse to never start. Just plug in your mic and start recording!

Our podcast became the ultimate funnel. We rarely if ever call out the service that we provide in the podcast. The podcast has become a nurturing mechanism at the top of the funnel and is one of the primary onramps to our ecosystem. We later learned that most people who end up purchasing our service had listened to our podcast for at least three months. It's a way to take a cold audience and let them get to know you, like you, and trust you. We talk a lot about why they need things in their agency that "coincidentally" is part of our offer. So, we give them a lot of the *what* and the *why* and occasionally sprinkle in the *how*.

Not only does it nurture people at the front end of our funnel, but it also encourages them even when they're in our program. Almost all our clients continue to listen to the podcast. It really helps to reinforce all the *why* we do what we do in our service. For many of the agents that have had success with our program, there's usually a rough start for the first couple months. The podcast helps their mindset by reinforcing why they're doing what they're doing, and provides hope and guidance during this time, keeping them going until they get results. In fact, a lot of people who have canceled their membership end up returning to us because they listened to the podcast and realized that they hadn't utilized everything we had to offer. They want to come back to do it right.

A podcast may not seem to be your jam, but the principles behind it are things I believe all businesses should do as an entry point. Your message needs to get out there, and for us, podcasts get a lot of our content to lots of people across many platforms. Just like Russell Brunson says, "Always be publishing." His constant publishing, writing, shooting, and stories are likely why we are all here at this conference, and why we made the decision to join the Funnel Hacker Tribe.

▶ **What is the greatest skill you needed to develop to be as successful as you are?**

As entrepreneurs, we move quickly and yet, we always seem to have our eye on the next idea that may have popped into our mind. With our flood of creativity and passion to execute our ideas, sometimes (maybe more than just sometimes), we can start so many different projects that our surroundings and to-do lists can be cluttered with incomplete work, leading to burnout and frustration.

Consistency is Key

We found that keeping a mental watchguard at the gates of creativity helps with relieving some of the excess "must-execute" energies. Being in the same room with so many high-performing visionaries in the Inner Circle community, as well as the broader ClickFunnels community, that creative energy can be enhanced, instead of tamed.

We had no way to stifle creativity as it poured out (or even a desire to do so), but the wave of inspiring ideas needed to be tamed. We live in a world that has taught us that instant gratification is something to expect, and as a result, our own mind's dopamine networks have been trained to seek activities and relationships that will yield instant results.

Yet, our logic center knows that there's no easy path. There is no easy answer and no "silver-bullet."

So with a sentry at our mind's creative center, and an understanding that we won't win Two Comma Awards with a quick idea or magic product, we understood that having a framework mattered, and consistent execution was key to every instance within our business, both to use the product we've created, and to distribute our product.

The greatest skill we've developed over our ongoing (and never ending) journey, has been consistency.

In our previous lives, our only focus was selling more insurance in our insurance agencies. We had yet to enter into the ClickFunnels community, but already we were showing the tenacity, and "outside-the-box" thinking and doing that marks Funnel Hackers.

We had gotten great at creating processes within our agencies and creating consistency around many different processes. Doing so allowed us to gain business leverage within our insurance agencies so that we'd be able to spend more time branching out into other business ventures.

At the time, prior to the podcast, we'd started to get plugged into a lot of insurance agency owners through Facebook groups (keep in mind, this is circa 2012). As we met more and more agents, we began to share more and more ideas between insurance agency owners. Prior to Facebook Groups, agency owners were on an island, and rarely had much, if any, interaction with their peers.

They were stuck in their world, grinding out 12 to 14-hour days, "fighting the good fight." The last thing we wanted to do was get into any fight, especially when it came to insurance. We had very little interest in the subject of insurance, were already bored and uninterested, and knew that we needed to create systems and processes that would unlock time so that we could focus our efforts on finding something more interesting to work on and be a part of.

We filled our days up with creating a process, applying the process, reviewing the results, and then adding it to the process manual. We certainly didn't want to mirror some big corporation with a process for everything, but we did want to make sure that the basics were covered, ensuring we had the freedom from our insurance to set out on other endeavors.

We took the best pieces of what other agents shared with us. Craig even tried and failed with a business that would serve to collate all of the agents' processes in one place, a Process Vault, which failed, but that's another story for another time.

Once we'd systematized our agencies, we had extra time. With that extra time, we created the podcast, which ended up being the ultimate stack, and all because we created a consistent process, and did not deviate—even 500 episodes later—it may actually hold true that besides waking up everyday, the podcast may be the most consistent activity we've ever done!

That podcast, and the consistent weekly publishing is what has led us to where we are today. We had two outcomes when we started: learn how to create predictable sales and help other agents by sharing this knowledge. The most interesting result was the series of events that resulted from pursuing those two outcomes.

We interviewed marketing leaders from many industries and the top insurance agents from around the country, and published two to three times a week. We took the knowledge we gained, then organized it into an overall framework which we then implemented. When we did this, we started to breakthrough on the sales side of the equation, reaching as high as Top Ten in sales production for the entire carrier (out of more than 14,000 agencies).

By being consistent with our learning and content creation, we had become successful in our primary businesses, which opened an opportunity to share our framework with other agents using the same podcast we had learned from. We had created an audience while at the same time developing the framework we'd later be selling to the people who were listening as we were building it! It was circular, and it was amazing.

One guest, Jamie Alderton, a fitness coach in England, shared a story where he'd passed this pull-up bar every morning while he was on his morning jog. He shared that he'd decided to do ten pull-ups every day when he passed this pull-up bar. He went on to share that he didn't notice anything the first day, the first week, or even the first few months. One year later though, he noticed how muscles he never worked were growing and well-defined, all because of the consistency behind doing those pull-ups.

This is what happened with the podcast: we didn't see anything from a revenue standpoint from our podcast until two years after we started. At this point, however, we were getting over 5,000 downloads a week and we had an audience. And it was not just an audience, but a highly interested, trusting, and well-understood avatar.

Now, we combined the marketing consistency we'd use to create our audience and the consistency of our new business acquisition process at our insurance agencies to deliver an incredible new opportunity for other insurance agencies. This would be one that allowed them to create consistency for themselves in their agencies with their sales funnels.

The fundamental trait across the board for all of the success we've managed to put together in the last five years has been *consistency* with what we do.

▶ **What was the greatest mindset or identity shift you had to have to be as successful as you are?**

For us, our peers are our avatar. In fact, we've come to realize that we are the perfect avatar for the services that we deliver. This realization has created a very interesting path for us to deliver our products and services.

Your Greatest Challenge Is Your Answer

Since our own insurance agencies are the perfect ecosystem to beta test our ideas and products in the development phase, we are able to more clearly understand the success potential our prospects will have based on the results we achieve. Instead of looking for a way around challenges as they present themselves, we know that the path to breakthrough success is *through*, not *around* the obstacles that get in the way.

We have become numb to the sting of failure, because at the "testing phase" we have an understanding that we won't always get it right. We've learned, however, that the path to our successful desired outcome is paved with many mistakes–and that's okay.

We push to make mistakes when we beta test a concept prior to doing a full-blown launch to our clients. If we can mitigate the "client facing" mistakes by first using our own agencies as incubators, it allows for more creativity and less disruption of our members' experiences.

For example, one of the many things we've included in our new opportunity is a myriad of lessons that, if applied correctly, will definitely help someone build out and obtain incredible results with their own TeleFunnel new client acquisition system.

We know this to be true because we tested all of the steps, metrics, and inputs for two years before even offering a tactical plan for agents. We spend all the time, energy, and human capital on first securing results within our insurance agencies. Then once we have proof of concept, we create an irresistible offer for our service and launch it.

In many cases, had we tested various offers by launching them first, and using agents' time and money to learn what works, we would have potentially burned too many opportunities. Our outcome is to ensure our clients get results. It's our mission to free them from being agency operators.

This isn't to say we shouldn't test various things directly with the audience, such as messaging, content, or other more forgiving activities, but again, the fear can paralyze people from getting started, or if they get started, from keeping consistent, and ultimately from obtaining results.

An amazing concept that gleaned from being part of this community and have taken to heart is the incredible mindset of abundance that is shared across the masses. This is especially prevalent in our Inner Circle coaching group. Unfortunately, our avatar doesn't always share this mindset of abundance.

Often, insurance agents who stumble into our world from an ad, group, or the podcast, can be new to this mindset and have limited resources, or they've been an insurance agent for so long, they are set in their ways. We know that the service we offer can help any agent to generate consistent results, but we've had to learn HOW through honing our deliverables' processes within our agencies, in order to ensure we deliver impactful results for our members once they've bought in.

We have created an offer that every insurance agent needs. We have continued to perfect the offer, making it so good that, compared to any other path the agent can take, they'd be crazy to choose anything else. We have tried to limit the amount of "convincing" that our offer requires in order to avoid having to persuade them into action. We all know delivering what they want versus convincing them of what they need is a faster, easier sale.

We fought through many obstacles to get our own agencies' versions of what we sell to clients airtight so that there's not a lot of wiggle room to veer off course, but none of it would be in place, had we not been transformed from a scarcity mindset to that of abundance. That mindset occurred from the close relationships we've developed in the Funnel Hacker Community. Even within the community we've created with insurance agents, we continue to reinforce the "journey" versus "destination" message, as we help agents understand that pain is part of the process.

Our new opportunity is "done with you," and we help to walk them through those failures. We help them understand that messing up is part of the process, and becoming "scarcity-driven" is a path to permanent failure versus taking micro-failures and using them as lessons from which we learn, grow, and push closer toward our desired goals.

As you embark on your journey to help service your niche, you may want to embrace failures as part of your own lesson book. While frustrating, and especially for right-brained, high "I" entrepreneurs, who have those visionary egos, the failures will provide valuable data that can be used to elevate and ignite future opportunities.

A great example of testing in our own agencies prior to sharing as a product or offer to our members/clients was lead numbers. We knew that if we wanted to provide accurate insights and recommendations to potential clients, we'd need cold, hard data or else we'd never be able to create a scalable business that could serve 1,000s of insurance agents.

So we invested in internet leads. We bought all kinds, from many different vendors. We didn't fear what would work or wouldn't work. We didn't fear the spend (well, maybe a little), and we knew from prior experiences (failures and wins) that we'd gain valuable insight into what worked, as well as being able to test and prove out our TeleFunnel framework.

We identified the KPIs and began to understand what acceptable and profitable results looked like and which results weren't good enough or weren't cost effective. We were also amazed that a lot of similar metrics from the online marketing world applied to the new opportunity we'd created.

We determined what ACV was needed, and in our clients' cases, the lifetime value of their sales (from our own insurance agencies' numbers), lead cost (CPL), and Cost Per Sale (CPS). The TeleFunnel we'd created gave us great insight into the results of the "traffic" (internet leads) any insurance agent could/would purchase and what type they should purchase.

We also gained valuable intel about quantity needed, the type of lead purchased, the number of dials needed, what kind of system to call with, and how these leads needed to be handled once our sales team was on the phone with them. It created predictability, and THAT my friends is what allows for scaling. All of this came from *overcoming the fear of failure*, the *fear of spending money*, the fear of just going for it.

I remember Jason asking me one time, "How much did you spend to go to college? Think of the lead spend we're doing now, of all these mistakes we are making, as a new college track that we are paying to learn from. Except, this is real coursework, real learning with real money in the real world." That stuck with me.

Learn we did! We created those benchmarks and have been able to change the lives of 100s of insurance agents by helping them sell more than they'd ever imagined they could, unlocking freedom for them, while at the same time taking us into a quantum leap through Russell's Inner Circle. If we had feared failure, or stopped at the first sign of frustration, we would still be on the phone with insurance clients helping them as the "business operator," who is actually the hardest working employee. Our stubborn resolve to help insurance agents break free, above and beyond all other goals, helped us grow into who we are. We hope you're inspired to dive in and help change your world!

www.theidudes.com

My Gold Nugget Takeaways

The Owners

Chapter 6

Erik Sorenson

Erik is an Entrepreneur, Podcaster, Author, Public Speaker, and Marketer. He grew up in Farmington Utah and attended Brigham Young University to study Marketing Communications. After BYU, Erik started an Advertising agency with no money and no experience and grew it to an 8 figure business working with Fortune 500 and 1000 companies including Walt Disney, TDS Telecom, Gold's Gym, The FBI, the US Air Force, USA Communications, Zion National Park, Bryce Canyon, and Moab to name a few. Since then has created 9 companies.

Erik sold his ad agency in 2017 and created a strategic growth company including, marketing, automation, and professional development. He then launched a transformational leadership and coaching program speaking to thousands of business leaders across the country to help them extract their potential, accelerate achievement and RISE to their potential.

In August of 2022 Erik's latest effort made the Inc. 5000 list of fastest growing companies in America. Erik has 10 children, he is a serial entrepreneur, marathon runner, Ironman triathlete, and an instrument-rated pilot.

▶ **What was the greatest piece of advice you received from a mentor or coach that made the biggest impact in your agency journey?**

My father was a highly respected businessman, the kind that many would seek out for advice. Growing up, I would have people come up to me all of the time telling me how sound his advice was and how much it changed their life. I had never really gone to him for advise when I was young, it was only when I came to make a major shifting point in my life that I sought his advice.

I was in the middle of making a decision to "burn the boats" by walking out of my good paying nine-to-five job and start my first agency and I desperately needed some direction from someone that had much more experience than I. We scheduled a lunch and I sat down with him. As I told him of my situation, he listened intently for a long time and then told me something that I would never forget; "Risk is always equal to reward." He repeated himself again:

"Risk is always equal to reward."

I'm not fully sure I understood the entirety of the concept at that time, but it wouldn't take long for me to discover exactly what he meant. After all, taking a risk can turn out to be a very positive or a very negative move.

I had a choice to make. I could stay in a comfortable low-risk job that would, over time, make good money, or I could follow a feeling that I was born for more, that I was meant to take a few steps into the darkness and change the world. I realized that there were no guarantees, but the amount of risk I was willing to take to do what I was born to do would pay off one way or another. At least that was my belief. I had to take the risk. I then made a decision that created an entirely new destiny. I quit the job and started my first agency.

I have heard it said many times that you are one decision away from breaking through to a very different future whether that be massive success in business or major shifts in your personal life. I found this to be very true. You literally are one decision from everything changing for the better. It takes a big amount of courage to make a decision like that and at some point you will have to make that type of decision. It would benefit you to make that decision sooner rather than later, knowing that the decision point will eventually come, and your future won't open up until you take such a risk.

Making this decision was like jumping off a cliff and finding my wings on the way down. I had very little education, almost no experience, no clients, no money, and no real plan. I had a dream, a vision to make my mark in the world and nothing was going to stop me from doing it. I knew it was a big risk and I took it.

It would take some time to fully realize the risk that I took, but it led to a long career in the agency space, a space that I still love and live today.

It led to me building an agency that would generate over $50 million in revenue, allow me to work with Fortune 500 and 1000 clients like Walt Disney, Kia Motors, the US Air Force, The FBI, Gold's Gym, USA Communications, and hundreds of others.

As a business owner, there is risk in everything that you do. It is humbling to know that it is all on you, that your paycheck isn't in any way guaranteed. But because most business owners are driven by the desire to make an impact in the world, it makes the risk seem a little less risky.

You can accomplish an incredible number of things if you are willing to be less risk-averse. In the game of owning a business, there is risk everywhere that can either paralyze you or lead you to your greatest moments. Taking a risky move is so hard to do because often you don't realize the outcome for weeks, months, or even years. There are no guarantees of success.

I think this is partly why entrepreneurs are such a rare breed. They are willing to take risks that could financially bankrupt themselves, but they do it all because they have a stronger "why" that usually goes far beyond money. I know for me, I invest money into the business in quantities that I would never invest in my personal life. I do this because I have the confidence that it will pay large dividends down the road and lead to my ultimate dream outcomes: impact and freedom.

Always remember that risk always equals reward so if you want a big reward, you must take a risk.

▶ **What would you say was the biggest contributing factor to your success?**

Because I had started an agency with little to no resources, I had to figure out a way to get clients and get them fast. I knew I couldn't use an extensive portfolio, I knew I couldn't talk about former results...I had none! I had to figure out a way to compete at the highest level without the resources of everyone else, and win.

I immediately started looking for where the agency space was being underserved. What holes could I find that existed in the current agency model and how could I fill a space that would make me stand out? Before I ventured off on my own, I worked as an advertising account manager so I had the blessing of working with agencies both big and small. I could see first hand decisions that were being made and look for opportunities.

After doing this for 2 years, I started to notice some holes. I saw agencies make decisions for their clients that weren't in the best interest of the client. Their choices were decisions that were clearly in the best interest of themselves. This bothered me.

I spoke to some of them about this and even brought new fresh ideas to the table. I looked for better ways to support them and the end client. I looked and suggested ways that would provide better results for their clients and make them look like a rockstar at the same time..This didn't go over well and I didn't understand why.

One of my co-workers said to me, "Erik, don't you know that agencies are where good ideas go to die?" This shocked me. An agency is where you get all of the answers, the best ideas, and incredible creative. They are supposed to be the best-of-the-best, full of ideas and proven strategies to help a client grow.

In this, I saw an opening to create a new opportunity and by making decisions that were in the best interest of the client and provide more value than anyone else was willing to provide as an agency owner. Because I didn't have the portfolio like other agencies nor the experience, I knew I would have to leverage the one talent that I did have: hustle.

I was willing to do what most weren't willing to do primarily because I didn't have a choice. It was either go at it with everything or die on the vine. I was bent on finding a way to the result no matter what it took. I was also relentless in focusing only on the client, their results, and I knew the money would eventually come. Well, it worked.

I hit the ground running, talking to any business that would listen to me. My inexperience and somewhat naive self didn't see limitations that others saw because it was all new to me and I didn't know the right way. I didn't know what I didn't know.

Then it happened. I got my first client, created a campaign for them, and launched it! I'll never forget the first payment I received from my first client of over $17,000. What surprised me most was how addicting it was to see a campaign that I created generate growth in my client's business. It was magical to me. That first move created momentum that grew my little agency from nothing to $1 million, then to $3 million, and within a few years, my agency was billing close to $10 million per year.

I started winning business that I, at the time, had no business winning. My clients saw something in me that they weren't seeing in others. I knew that it was all on my shoulders so I had to succeed or my family and I would not eat.

I became known for finding effective solutions to any problem a client had. I even changed my voice mail to the following: "Hi, you've reached the phone of Erik Sorenson. If you're a client, whatever the question is, the answer is yes." (Since those early days, I have gotten a lot wiser and learned that saying no is just as important).

Our clients would bring us problems and we would figure out a way to solve them even if we had never encountered the problem before or had any experience. Erik, can your team build us a website? Of course." Erik can you produce video? "Yes." Erik, can you wrap 375 of our vehicles in 7 states? "No problem." (This was a real request and we got it done).

Your clients must see something in you that they don't see in others. They must have confidence that you are more likely to get them to their dream outcome than anyone else. You must be fully committed to the client and create a perception that you can get them to the result, then make that perception a reality.

Until results start to come, the client is buying you. It helps to have social proof to help build confidence in your ability to get results but even when you have the case studies, they are still buying you.

There was a study that came out a few years ago as to the top reasons why people hire an agency. When I first read the study, I immediately assumed that increased results and/or growth was the #1 reason why a client would hire an agency but I was wrong. It was time. For the business owner, they don't have time to run the business, generate customers through sales, do payroll, manage the books, try to be profitable, and execute marketing. Time is the big issue and time is why the agency gets hired.

Clients will pay for speed. They just want to focus on what they want to focus on and have an agency make it rain customers so they can get to the result as fast as possible. They often don't want to have to deal with marketing and the time it takes to do it the right way.

Today more than ever, things are changing at an unprecedented rate. Algorithms are changing, audience perceptions are changing, consumer habits are shifting, and it is becoming harder and harder to reach the ideal client. Agencies play a critical role in keeping up with the everchanging world and finding the right strategies to capture the right audience.

Most business owners don't have time to figure it all out, so they need you, the agency. How often did Russell Brunson mention hiring an agency from stage during FHL 2021? He mentioned it over and over because even he, as an expert marketer, knew his time was better spent on all the required efforts to make a campaign successful. *He* didn't commandeer placing ads on social media or other digital platforms. Agencies remove the burden of time and allow the client to be more product and customer focused while their ad campaigns are running correctly. You want to grow exponentially? Solve their problem of time.

▶ **What is the greatest skill you need to develop to be as successful as you are?**

There are two major skills that are required in order to be a successful agency owner.

1. Be a good communicator
2. Be 100% focused on client results

Remember that the real battle of marketing is not about products or services; it's about perceptions. You are creating perceptions about a product or service that will lead to a purchase. This can only happen if you can first create a perceived likelihood of achieving the dream outcome of the consumer. Of course, to do that, you must know what their dream outcome is.

This is also true when acquiring new clients for yourself. That is why you must be a good communicator and have the confidence to create a perception that you are the answer, that you can solve the problem and bring the client's dream outcome to them faster than anyone else can. This is why so many of us generate as much social proof as possible, to create the perception that, "f I can get all of these people to their dream outcome, I can get you there too."

When you are first trying to gain new clients, the way you speak will either boost or kill confidence in the client's perceptions of what you can do for them. This is true whether or not you are speaking in person, through a funnel, or through email communications. Your future client's perception is their reality. The world is never the way it actually is; the world is the way your client *thinks* it is.

A few years ago, we pitched what for us was a large client. Their marketing spend was around $85,000 per month and we started reaching out to them to set up a meeting. Unfortunately, it didn't happen for a while. A client that size wasn't going to just take a meeting from us since we didn't previously have a relationship. It took over a year of continuously reaching out to finally get them to say yes to a meeting. This was a big enough deal that we hopped on a plane to pitch them what we could do for them and why they should hire us as an agency. Through our discovery, we discovered a few things. First, they were just coming out of some rough years and were willing to invest more into growth. Second, the company was worth about $20 million at the time, and they were looking to grow with the goal of eventually selling. Last, they were looking at a complete rebrand to a name and identity that would connect better with consumers.

Knowing this, we went in with unique strategies and ideas to solve the challenges they were facing, take the marketing burden from them, and help them achieve their growth goals. In reality, they were just looking for someone they trusted to get them across the finish line of their growth goals.

The client said *yes* and hired us to oversee all aspects of marketing. Since this would be our largest client, we dove in fully. We studied every market they were in, interviewed their customers to deeply understand their ideal client, created focus groups, and dug deep into every metric that they could give us so that we could make better decisions that would lead to their growth. We spent countless hours in research that ended up paying off down the road when we launched their campaigns.

They grew…and grew…and grew. The grew so much so that they started acquiring other companies. 4 years later, that client sold their business for $265 million. That's a 13x of their original valuation. Of course, when this happened, I was crazy excited for them but worried that we would also be losing our biggest client. We quickly found out that since we had put so much into growing their business and had provided so much value that the company who had acquired them took notice. This Fortune 1000 company requested a meeting with us and we jumped at the chance to continue to work with them. I'll never forget the meeting and how nervous I was. Was I about to lose my biggest and favorite client or was I about to gain a much bigger client in the process?

It was like we were pitching all over again like we did in the beginning. During that meeting and in and subsequent conversations, they saw something in us and hired us on to handle their marketing. This client was much larger than our former client which led to even more growth in our agency.

Word of this success spread, and we ended up gaining millions of dollars of new business just because of this one massive success. It truly put us on the map.

My relationship with the original client still exists today. In fact, the other day the owner posted on my LinkedIn page the following; "By the way, you are one heck of a good leader that inspires the best in people!"

The #1 most important skill is to be a good communicator. You must be a good communicator in order to be successful in the agency business. I am talking about your ability to communicate value *to* the client and your ability to communicate value *on behalf of* the client. The agency world has two faces. The first is that of growing your *agency* and the second of growing your *client*. You must be able to communicate value to acquire new clients and to grow your client's business. That is why this skill is so valuable.

Fortunately, one of my strengths is the ability to communicate and create perceptions that I and my team can get a client to their dream outcome. This always came easy to me and was a talent that made it much easier to grow a strong client list. If you aren't born with this skill, do your best to develop it or find a 'who' that can do it for you.

The #2 most important skill is to be laser focused on getting results for your client. Nothing else matters. You can have the most beautiful looking ads, the most incredible funnels, with copy that sounds amazing, but if it doesn't produce results, it doesn't matter.

Results are what really matters in the agency space, period.

This also places emphasis on why you must clearly know the dream outcome of your client and make sure it's completely realistic so expectations are aligned with the results you know you can produce.

I recently created a new agency in the healthcare space and I now ask our clients to judge us on one metric and one metric alone. How many patient appointments did we get for you? Clicks, impressions, and reach doesn't matter if you can't generate the lead, appointment, or sale. That is the only thing that matters.

Even though we have a complete real-time results dashboard, the only metric we talk about is how many appointments they gained from our marketing programs and how many of them converted.

▶ **What was the greatest mindset or identity shift you had to have to be as successful as you are?**

A few years ago, I had an opportunity to meet with an astronaut that taught me something that I would never forget. His name was Senator Jake Garn from the State of Utah. He was a highly decorated Navy pilot and had accumulated over 15,000 flight hours in his long and distinguished career. Now if you know anything about being a pilot, very few ever come close to accumulating that many hours. This guy had a massive amount of experience flying airplanes!

I drove to the airport on a Saturday morning to meet him. As I drove up to his hanger, I could see his airplane inside as well as a few personal items. As I walked into his hangar the first thing I noticed was a very large photograph that spanned the 100-foot hangar wall. It looked like a billboard, it was so big.

It was a photo of him while he was taking a space walk outside the space shuttle Discovery during his seven day orbit. It was breathtaking. Inside of his hanger he had an older North American Navion airplane. It was a small 4-seater airplane that he likely flew when he was in the Navy many years prior. He seemed very fond of the airplane and flew it every week to keep up on his skills.

I, being a pilot, was intrigued by the airplane. It was in perfect shape considering the age. As I walked up to it, Mr. Garn told me to step into the plane and look at the cockpit. Being a pilot, everything inside was immediately familiar to me yet I was asked a simple question that to this day I remember vividly.

Mr. Garn turned to me and said, "Erik, do you know why I'm alive today?"

I wasn't sure exactly why he was asking the question and I promptly replied, "Why is that?" He then instructed me to look at a booklet that was sitting on the pilot seat. I immediately recognized what it was. It was a book that I had used countless times in the many flights I had piloted over the years. It was a book that I used during every flight, every time. The book was a checklist for every procedure required to successfully fly the airplane from start to finish.

It included procedures of what to do in pre-flight, what to do before you start the engine, what to do on taxi, take off, ascent, cruise, decent, switching fuel tanks, and the list goes on and on. The most important aspect of the checklist is the section that contains emergency procedures. If there is an in-flight fire, there is a procedure. If you lose an engine, there is a procedure. If you lose electrical power, there is a procedure. There is a procedure for anything and everything that could go wrong when in flight written down in a step-by-step format, one by one. During flight school you train on these procedures over and over and learn to know most of them by flight and yet, you still use the checklist.

He then turned to me and said, "I'm alive today because of that checklist. No matter how many times I've flown this airplane or countless other aircraft, I have always used the checklist every time and it has kept me alive to this day. I've flown thousands of flights, I have those checklists memorized, and yet I still go through them one by one to make sure I am following the exact procedure to have a successful flight, every time."

When you are flying it is literally life or death. If you make a mistake, it could cost you your life. On the many flights that I have piloted, I was obsessed with following each item in order because I knew what the consequences were if I didn't. The order in which the procedures are followed is critical and must be followed exactly to be successful.

When you follow the proven procedures, you stay alive. When you follow proven procedures, your *business* stays alive.

Using a checklist of procedures wasn't natural for me as a business owner. My strategy was ready, fire, aim! Unlike when flying an airplane, there are no procedures that exist when you first start a business…you must create them. Having them can be the difference between you staying in business or going out of business. Even though I hated creating SOP's, I loved them when they were complete and implemented. It made everything so much easier.

What if your SOP's guaranteed success, if they were followed in order? What if you had emergency procedures for when things don't go as planed? What if you had a simple checklist that, when performing a business function, you could simply pick up the checklist and execute it one item at a time?

The truth is, you already do have some. *Expert Secrets* and *Traffic Secrets* are two invaluable checklists that every agency must study. It literally contains checklists (frameworks) that if followed consistently and continually optimized, it will lead you to success.

What Astronaut Jake Garn taught me that day was life-changing. Without SOP's, I could only hustle my way so far. I could never get past the $10 million per year mark in my business. Years later in a conversation I had with Garrett J. White, he told me that most people can hustle their way to $10 million, but can't get past that number without building a team and implementing SOP's. He was right and Mr. Garn was right.

It was hard for me to stop being busy and start working smarter. Busyness is a form of laziness. It keeps you moving so you feel like you are putting in the work, but you aren't putting in the *right* work. It's the results that actually matter, not how much you hustled to get there. Creating and implementing SOP's will save massive amounts of time and help you do the right thing, every time.

What Mr. Garn taught me that day was an invaluable lesson on how to stay alive in business both in the present and for years to come.

I can still hear his wise words today, "I'm alive because of that checklist."

For more information visit: **ErikSorenson.com**

My Gold Nugget Takeaways

The Owners

Chapter 7
Andrea Peer

Andrea is an uber nerd on all things customer experience. After 18 years designing, researching, and building software products for customers around the world in companies ranging from Fortune 50 to small start-ups, she decided to venture into the world of entrepreneurship. In addition to her PhD, she added certifications and training in Funnel Hacking, Design Hacking, Game Thinking, and Tiny Habits to her Ph.D. in Human Computer Interaction. With this arsenal of education and experience, Andrea developed her Journey Crafting framework and the Customer Keeper Method. Journey Crafting is how to design and build transformative customer experiences that delight, surprise, and honor our humanness. The Customer Keeper Method is a systematic way to build customer experiences that result in customers showing up, investing, and returning. Today, she is busy guiding purpose-driven coaches, course creators, experts, and SaaS owners to revolutionize the customer experience they offer through DIY, DWY, and DFY Journey Crafting services. And even more specifically, she currently is applying the Customer Keeper Method to programs that are trying to grow from $3M to $10M+ and want to stop the leaky bucket, waning engagement problem. When she is not geeking out on experiences and customer retention, she enjoys the beauty of the Pacific Northwest with her friends, family, and 4 cats.

My name is Andrea Peer, CEO and Founder of the Customer Keeper Method. I help course creators, coaches, and SaaS owners build memberships, courses and programs that inspire customers to do three things: 1) show up 2) invest and 3) stay.

My clients help people elevate their consciousness and step into bigger versions of themselves. And my agency helps these passionate, heart-centered entrepreneurs reimagine their offers, leverage data, and use research-based methods to drive human behavior. The goal? To keep customers from drifting away forever.

On any given day, you can find me with a cat in my lap, and a Starbucks in my hand, turning ideas into realized dreams using customer journey mapping techniques and a whole host of technology, ClickFunnels being a major part in that tech stack..of course.

But before we get too far, I need to tell you how I met Russel Brunson. (Hint: it involved copious amounts of mayonnaise.)

▶ How Russell Brunson and I Met on the Graveyard Shift

I started listening to Russell when I worked the midnight shift making sandwiches. But we'll come back to that in a second.

Midnight sandwich making or not, I should mention that I'm a supernerd. I have a PhD in Human Computer Interaction with 18 years' experience in the SaaS world researching, designing, and building digital product experiences.

During my time in Corporate America, the focus was always to: be the best and be competent...with an undercurrent of if you can't get the job done, then get out of my way.

I'm not proud to admit it but that philosophy fueled my success: I climbed the ladder to senior Vice President for some of the biggest companies in the world. The price I paid– which I think many of us do– was extreme disconnection from anyone...including myself.

In 2017 a friend invited me to the Sacred Valley in Peru and through a series of events, I was put face to face with what the future held if I continued my current path of disconnection. In that moment, I woke up and allowed spirit/God/Universe in. When I returned home, I started my transition from Corporate to entrepreneurship.

I was committed to walking a different path. Which was all well and good....but my severance from leaving Silicon Valley had run out. (Hence the reason I was slapping mayo on bread, and driving Lyft® so that I could take classes and programs during the day.)

The good news is, in one of my programs, I discovered Russell Brunson. So, it wasn't long and Russell started coming with me to work.

And so it began:

- ♦ Deep Experts became the soundtrack to mayo on bread.

- ♦ Funnology kept me company as I put ham and muenster on rye.

- ♦ Dot Com Secrets curled up in my brain as I placed shredded lettuce on subs.

Glamorous I know, right?

So how do you go from minimum wage sandwich making to $20-30k months in your agency? Well, it starts with showing up.

▶ Tip #1: Show Up.

Two months after Russell came into my life, I knew I had to be in the room at Funnel Hacking Live. I had no money but I was determined to get there.

I scraped together the last few airline points I had and I showed up with a backpack full of PowerBars® and $10 a day for food (because a friend had lent me $100).

But the point is: I showed up. I got in the room. And what happened inside that room would fundamentally change the trajectory of my entrepreneurial journey.

I furiously took notes, I met people. I felt inspired. It was how I came in first contact with Kathryn Jones, a critical mentor and guide for me.

And then on day 4, Russell invited us to join 2CCX. In his brilliantly delivered invitation, in addition to the amazing program he laid out, he said two magic things - (1) I didn't have to pay for 30 days, and (2) there was a free lunch after you signed up.

As soon as the invitation was extended, I was walking to the table in the back to join. Without having ANY idea how I was going to pay for it, I signed up for the Two Comma Club (Something, despite all practical logic I have been able to pay for and participate in every month since).

When I saw all the food at the lunch, I felt a rush of relief. (It had been a longgggg week of eating PowerBars). But quickly after the food had been consumed, reality set in. Not having had any real wins in the entrepreneurial space yet and not even being able to pay for this invitation, I didn't feel like I belonged in the room so I retreated to the bathroom. It was super nice and I didn't even feel like I belonged in the dang bathroom!

After hiding in the bathroom stall, getting my bearings, I pushed past my discomfort and went back into the main room with fellow 2CCX folks and just started talking to people.

It wasn't hard after that day to find and surround myself with cool people in the ClickFunnels community. I went to trainings. I networked and connected with as many people as possible.

And while I did spend the next six months slapping mayo on bread—something was fundamentally different: my agency was in motion. And it felt amazing.

And here's the main point….I want to be real with you: 90% of my clients come from the connections I've made in the Two Comma Club. 100% of my business comes from word of mouth. It was and continues to be these connections that make the difference for me.

Before long, I was able to leave the sandwich shop. In the second year of my business, I consistently started having $20-30k months.

▶ **Tip #2: Say Yes Until…**

The biggest contributing factor to my success has been saying yes. Showing up. Allowing myself to be seen- even when it didn't feel comfortable. Going for it…even when I wasn't sure how in the heck I was going to pay for it… even when I had to stay in a $30 Airbnb® (sketchy!) and eat PowerBars all week.

Say yes to the opportunities in front of you.

This has helped me connect with so many new people. Saying yes helped me do right by people. It also helped me find people who were willing to stick with me in the long haul.

So, I embrace the philosophy of saying yes....until it's time to say no. You get to gauge the "no" based on your own experience, of course. I am now at a point in my agency work that I have started to say "no" more. No to the clients that aren't a good fit, no to the projects that are outside of our expertise, and most importantly, no to when my gut says, 'not this one.'

It has taken me 3 years to get to the point of saying no more. That being said, I still say yes more times than not. It has led me to amazing places!

▶ Tip #3: Soothe Your Ego and Learn

In Corporate America, bravada, confidence, and sweeping in with allll the answers is what wins.

As an agency owner in the entrepreneurial space, soothing your own ego long enough to hear other people's wisdom is what wins. What wins is being seen. What wins is daily re-focus. What wins is being on the phone to ClickFunnels support every day. Telling them, "Talk to me like I know nothing about ClickFunnels" (even though I've built hundreds of funnels).

What wins is being humble and being willing to learn. It's believing that everyone can teach you something.

▶ Tip #4 Choose Your Own Adventure (In Your Agency)

Choose the type of agency that fits you best. There are 3 major types of agencies.

1. **The "Order Taker" Agency**: How this goes is: the customer has a request, they send it to you and you deliver. Like a baton handoff. You don't have to have an ongoing relationship or a lot of meetings. It's convenient, the price point is lower...though the quality may sometimes be a little less. The client is paying for speed and convenience.

2. **The "Genius Design" Agency**: This is when you are super talented. The customer tells you the problem they are trying to solve, and you go off and do the work. There isn't a lot of engagement. You can charge very high rates without a lot of client

management, but you have to ensure that you can actually deliver to that high standard. In this model, the client is paying for hands off, high end, done for you, top dollar expertise.

3. **The "Co-Creation" Agency**: This is where you know the problem space and the technology. And your customer is the expert in their industry. You can develop holistic solutions together. Boundaries can be hard to set and not all clients are ready for the collaboration. But if you love to collaborate, it's a great option. (This is the structure of my agency.) In this model, clients pay for expertise, done with and for you services, and essentially a coach/confidant/support system that is willing to climb into the trenches with them.

To be clear, there isn't a right or wrong choice here. Start with where you are.

* Do you like to collaborate? If so, maybe a "The Co-Creation" Agency is for you.

* Do you like to work alone? Perhaps The "Order Taker" or The "Genius Design" Agency is more your speed.

But pick one and roll with it. (PS. Don't stress out about it too much. You can always change your mind later too).

▶ **Tip #5 Autonomy & Systems**

One of the best investments I ever made to help was a VIP day with a project manager who shared my values about the importance of a customer-centric approach. The investment with her was well spent– $1500 and 6 hours later, I felt my business stabilize in a whole new way– ready for the next level.

During our time together, we established every task and every step for each of my offerings and put it into ClickUp. The result? Projects went so smoothly from kickoff to close…because everything was now mapped out. The process helped my team understand every step and the efficiencies we've gained have been incredible. It doesn't matter if it's ClickUp, or some other tool, carve out the time to map out each step of every offer you have.

Tip #6 Three Things That'll Save You Some Headaches

→ **Standardize your offerings as quickly as possible.**
When I started, I wanted to do custom builds for everyone. Which is really cool but also super inefficient…and not easy to scale. So think about it like a sandwich shop- pick a set number of offerings that you know are good– and stick to those. (You can always throw in something a little extra when you need to.)

→ **Make sure your offerings are solid before you add new ones.**
Can I tell you how this is a lesson I learned the HARD way? The result: A lot of unnecessary frustration. Get your offerings solid before you chase something new. (You can thank me later on this one!). You're probably crazy talented at a lot of things but taking it on because you can figure it out is not a reason to do it. If you do want to add on services, find a willing beta client and try it once. Then decide if you are going to scale it or drop it.

→ **Follow your Gut.**
I know, I know: this is cliche. But seriously: Every. Single. Time. I've not trusted my gut when it came to a client, it turned out to be miserable and/or a real kick in the pants. So listen to your intuition. You have it for a reason.

▶ **Tip #7 Focus on Getting It Right Rather Than Being Right**

After I had my business for a few years, I had worked with one of my clients for months– building out a funnel and coaching membership experience for his customers. We were in deep.

HIs customers were getting fantastic results, he had solid traffic, but we had major struggles with conversion. We checked all the boxes in terms of fixing the funnel– A/B split testing, copy changes, all of it. No dice. We literally did everything we knew and a bunch of innovative strategies.

One day, his team told me that they wanted to use another funnel builder.

The old me–the Corporate Me–would have gone full on defensive to "save" the contract. She would have dug her heels in and convinced them to do it HER way. However, instead of being upset, or defending my abilities, I decided it was better to get it right than be right. I wanted to see him win, even if it meant I wasn't going to be the one to do it. So I rolled with it.

Was it hard? Um, yeah.

Did I have to soothe my ego some? Absolutely.

But do you know what happened? I continued to be a part of the team and supported the team in getting existing customers to stay. I was offered 20 percent equity in his business. I got amazing referrals and learned life-changing lessons. (I should mention that the other agency didn't get it right, either. But that isn't the point!)

The point is, when you put your ego aside and focus on getting it right instead of being right, doors open.

▶ Tip #8 On Birth and Birds (This Is A Big One!)

Your days will get busy. Your calendar fills up. In the midst of the hustle and bustle remember one thing:

Your business is birthing YOU as much as you are birthing your BUSINESS. Give yourself grace. Be patient.

Similarly, give space to your clients' learning process as well. Make room for them personally...not just the business they are building. Hold space for it to unfold. Understand that these things take time. The best things do!

Practice grounding. Don't steamroll for results when there needs to be a pause for contemplation, reflection, course-correction or a reset.

Honoring people first might mean we have uncomfortable situations. At times, it might mean prioritizing people over deadlines. But it means recognizing something important. It doesn't matter what we are doing if the people get forgotten in the process.

As conscious entrepreneurs who are here to do things a different way, we have to remember that there's room for it all. That there's success when people and processes come together in a beautiful way. If we just allow it... and stay open to it. And as you move through your days one thing is really important to remember:

You and your clients are like two wings of a bird.

This is an analogy my friend who is a CMBT therapist gave me. It stuck with me. She said, "You have no control of the other wing. But you have to learn how to fly together."

As agency owners, it's a constant journey of: Where does my wing end? Am I reaching into the other wing? How do we move together? How can we give and take…and ascend?

But when we honor people first. When we say yes and show up. When we start scrappy, right where we are (mayo not required). When we focus on soothing our ego and make our focus getting it right…

We commit to growth in new ways— which helps us soar. And together, we reach new heights.

Freebie link: https://customerkeepermethod.com/fhl-2022-agency-freebie

My Gold Nugget Takeaways

Chapter 8
Tyler Jorgenson

Since the age of five, I've been creating products and selling them. I love the process of creating and marketing physical products that customers can hold and use. In the age of the digital download and ebook, I help physical product sellers diversify revenue, develop new products and increase profits.

Over the years I have helped launch or worked on apparel brands, fitness equipment companies, subscription boxes, Amazon® stores, restaurants (that's another story), cosmetics, nutraceuticals, wellness products and more. My team and I have developed entire product lines for a national chain, one-off products for boutique sellers and just about everything you can imagine in-between. In the process I became a three-time 2 Comma Club Award Winner.

Hi, My name is Tyler Jorgenson and I'm an entrepreneur. It sounds like the intro to a support group but as far back as I can remember, I have loved solving problems and starting businesses.

I am a California based entrepreneur with an MBA from USC and I host a weekly radio show on ABC News Radio called BizNinja Entrepreneur Radio. I am a family man with four kids and, just once, a reality show contestant.

During my entrepreneurial journey I have owned a restaurant, multiple fitness centers, a real estate company, a mortgage firm, many retail websites and developed dozens of products sold in retail stores around the world.

Currently I run Four Sail, a digital marketing agency that works with physical product brands to diversify revenue and increase clients' business valuation.

▶ **What was the greatest piece of advice you received from a mentor or coach that made the biggest impact in your agency journey?**

Years ago, I was reading a post on Facebook from Perry Belcher where he mentioned that a lot of entrepreneurs shy away from agencies or service provider businesses because they think they are harder or more expensive than other types of businesses. He went on to explain that they really aren't very different but instead of machine cost, equipment cost or manufacturing cost, you have team cost and SOPS. My big takeaway from this was that as long as you approach an agency the same way you approach manufacturing, then you have the ability to create predictable output.

Since I had come from the manufacturing and product production world, this made a lot of sense to me. One of the biggest challenges was finding people who bought into the bigger vision and wanted to follow the process. Sometimes the people that we have on our team in the early days are not the right people to go to the next level of business.

Perry's advice showed me that agency work had the same potential for profits as other businesses and led me to working through problems the same way I would have worked through problems in product development.

▶ **What would you say was the biggest contributing factor to your success?**

It has been very interesting for me to see how many people start an agency doing something that they have very little experience in. It wouldn't necessarily be a problem if they were hiring and their focus was on operations. However, for most of the struggling agencies that I see, there is a major gap in understanding the whole business.

One of my agency's primary niches is in e-commerce. We help physical product owners diversify revenue and increase sales across multiple channels. For me this was a natural niche for us to serve since I had scaled and built multiple businesses using all of the services that we now provide to others.

I have never liked the saying *business is business*. It seems that people use this saying to justify making shady decisions. To me all business is personal. Whenever I go into a business deal, I approach it as a human and use contracts and communication to ensure clarity. I ask myself a few questions with any client.

- Do I believe that I can actually help this client?
- Do I believe this client has a chance to be successful with our services?
- Do I want to work with this client?
- Will this client be easy for my team to work with?
  - Are they coachable?
  - Are they teachable?
  - Are they accountable?

If I can overlay my years of experience and my team's skills on top of a brand with growth potential that is led by a business owner who is taking personal accountability, then we have the beginnings of the recipe for success.

▶ **What is the greatest skill you needed to develop to be as successful as you are?**

In many ways my agency was an accident. I had multiple brands that I was running that I owned and we had a few clients on the side just through friends and networking. When I sold off my brands, the natural move was to begin operating as an agency and bringing on more clients. In the beginning it seemed almost too easy. Clients were coming on as fast as I could grow the team. But we hit a point when, all of a sudden, networking and referrals wasn't enough.

We started creating offers and running ads and our pipeline started to fill up. The clients coming from ads come with a very different mindset than clients coming from a referral, so the sales process is different. The onboarding process is different. It is not that the actual process is different, but the need to resell, coach, and indoctrinate during the first 30 and 60 days is much higher.

The number one skill I needed to develop to grow and become more successful was to understand that both sales and marketing, and networking and referrals had to be mutually developed. The goal for our agency is to always have a pipeline full of clients ready to proceed so that we can grow not only substantially faster than attrition but as fast as our team can expand and support.

▶ **What was the greatest mindset or identity shift you had to have to be as successful as you are?**

Long before Alex Hormozi was the king of entrepreneur reels on Instagram, he and I were working on a project together. Right at the beginning of GymLaunch Alex, Leilah and I were driving around Dallas on our way to a dinner with a bunch of people from Russel Brunson's Inner Circle. GymLaunch was in its infancy then, and in many ways still just a dream for Alex and Leilah. From the back of the Uber®, Alex said something that, although we all agreed on, he took massive action to show its validity. He mentioned that it takes the same amount of energy to grow a 1 million dollar business as it does a 10 million dollar business. You put in the same amount of time, the same amount of energy, and the same amount of work, so you might as well build businesses with bigger potential.

I believe that this is true well beyond the 10 million dollar valuation.

Shortly after this conversation I watched as Alex made hard decisions to stay focused on his goal of turning the fitness marketing industry upside down. His advice to me through that time period was crucial.

One thing that Alex said to me during a particularly deep conversation about some of my current ventures, was that "your future is worth far more than your past."

If you find yourself working in a low-level opportunity, no amount of hard work and time is going to fix the opportunity.

It's not that you work any harder or put in more energy into a larger opportunity. It usually just comes down to the fact that the market can support a greater opportunity with more results.

We all have limiting beliefs and we all have paradigms that we have bought into. I remember the first time I saw people making seven figures per year. It changed my entire perspective of six-figure income being the target, but there are levels to paradigms. My biggest piece of advice is this:

Expand your thinking and get into circles you operate in and paradigms far greater than you can ever imagine, because if you're going to do the work of being an entrepreneur,
if you're going to go to the sacrifice of building your own business, you might as well play big.

www.tylerjorgenson.com

My Gold Nugget Takeaways

Chapter 9
Damon Burton

Over a decade ago, this husband and father of three beat a billion-dollar company by outranking their website on Google. Since then, he knew he was onto something and went on to build SEOnational.com, an international search engine marketing company that's worked with NBA teams, and Inc 5000 and Shark Tank featured businesses.

Having started his business right before the 2008 recession, Damon is familiar with navigating and growing a business through times like today, including tripling revenue during the recent pandemic. Never before has there been so many people needing something to focus their attention on, AND the time to do it.

I've learned more from knowing what people have done wrong than from any advice I have been given or from seeing what others have done right. The last two employers I had before I started my agency are good examples.

The first gentleman was incredibly successful. He did somewhere around $2 million a month. Other than a part-time secretary, I was his only full-time employee. He brought the relationships, and I did the work, but I made only $12 an hour. The pay wasn't even the issue, though. At the time, I didn't know my worth and thought the rate was fair.

Toxicity. That was the lesson to be learned.

Half a dozen others joined the team as the company grew, and it was time for a company Christmas party. He planned for the team to meet at a nightclub. His pitch was that he reserved a VIP table for the team. When we got there, we quickly realized that nothing was planned, and the VIP table was because he was there to hang out with his friends. He ditched us, asking the team to meet back at his room later.

My wife and I went and did our own thing and had a good night. Later on, we went back and met up at his room. We knocked on the door. He opened up with an odd smile, and we walked in.

Inside was friends only, no team members. Not knowing any of the others in the room, I walked forward with my eyes focused on the back of the room.

At the back of the room, my wife nudged me. After the second or third nudge, I realized she was guiding me to look toward the center of the room. The couch full of people I had passed were all doing cocaine on the center table.

My boss noticed that we noticed. He came up and rhetorically asked, "Everything cool?"

"Yep," I said. "You're good. We're going to head back to our room."

He repeated, "Everything's cool, right?"

We let them do their thing. We went and did our thing.

Somewhere around the same time of year, performance bonuses were due. Everyone on the team had been incentivized to meet some goals. The rewards were cash bonuses. The deadline went by. No bonuses were paid.

Somebody else on the team needed that money and raised their voice. The next thing I knew, the boss stormed out of the office, came back 20 minutes later, walked into my office, threw a few hundred dollars on the table and condescendingly said, "There's your bonus," as he turned his back and walked out.

Moments like that taught me about compassion and loyalty. It's not just about commitment from the employee to employer, but also vice versa, employer loyalty to employees.

Unfortunately, he didn't treat his family much better than his team. He had an amazing wife, who I still stay in touch with today. Their kids, who were all younger than ten, are now grown and off to college.

He frequently talked about his neighborhood and how their form of "keeping up with the Joneses," beyond traditional materialistic competition, was an open culture in the neighborhood of cheating on spouses.

From him, I learned how *not* to treat others. He's now divorced, and I've been happily married for 16 years. He often missed his kids' activities, while I've never missed a game or dance. He had a toxic workplace that no one wanted to stay in, while I've never had an employee quit and have been asked to be a godfather to team members' children... twice.

I've even been asked to attend a wedding. And when I couldn't make it because my wife was nearing delivery of our daughter, they ordered a life-size cardboard cutout of me from a sign company. They took the cutout to the wedding. Funny and inspiring at the same time, the emotions behind someone willing to have a cardboard representation of another person at their wedding says a lot. Six years after the wedding, I continue to get updates about "Cardboard Damon" still living the good life today. Lately, they've shared pictures of him gardening and playing guitar.

After the successful campaigns I designed for that boss, I was fortunate to have built up a reputation for results. When the goal was 300 conversions a day for his competitors, we would often hit 3,000.

When I left, word got around.

There was another gentleman who was starting a similar agency. He had come from another successful business, saw the money these other guys were making, and wanted to start his own agency in that space.

When he found out I quit, he contacted a mutual contact. I remember walking in my backyard when my phone rang. I answered "hello," and the mutual contact said, "Hey, I heard you're no longer with our old friend. Are you looking for another job?"

I told him I took a traditional nine-to-five job just to escape the toxicity, but I'd be open to a different opportunity. He says, "Great! I have a guy who is starting a similar agency. Are you available to talk to him... right now?

He got the other guy on the line, then bridged the call, and the guy offered me a job on the spot.

Living in Utah, he wanted me to move to Las Vegas. I told him no. I wasn't interested for a couple of reasons. One reason was the cost-benefit. He would pay me significantly more, at least relative to the times, which equated to $15,000 to $20,000 a year more. However, the cost-of-living difference between my city and Vegas netted out to around zero.

I also knew that kids were on the horizon for my wife and me, and I just didn't have an interest in raising a family in Las Vegas. He said "fair enough," and allowed me to work at home. Working from home proved not only flexible but also exposed an opportunity I'll share later in this chapter that helped me pivot into starting my agency.

Very different from the last company, the new one was great to work for. Though I worked remotely, you could feel that everyone was optimistic, they were family-first people, and it was a true team full of mutual respect among co-workers. Once a month, they'd fly me in, where I could feel the love and hunger for success even greater in person.

This employer was a lot different than the last guy. He had a storybook life. In his high school days, he was captain of the baseball team, he married the head cheerleader, and they had a handful of kids. He'd interrupt meetings to take his wife's call. Family was always first. But here's where I learned from him:

Don't be greedy.

The "successful company" that made him wealthy before his new company had lost a civil suit for millions of dollars. A few years later, the criminal case caught up.

Back in the days of AOL Instant Messenger, I was trying to contact the rest of the design team. No one was replying. I tried calling the landline at the office. Nobody answered there either.

"Did you hear?" Someone messaged me hours later. They went on to tell me that the FTC raided the company. They also had friends. Some other law enforcement agency was with them, too, because they literally kicked down the door to the building with guns.

It took me a few hours to finally get a hold of a manager in another department. They confirmed that the company was raided but offered some comfort and said, "Everything is fine. You're in a different department. You'll still get your paycheck this Friday."

At that moment, I had three choices.

1. Wait to see if my job still existed and if I would indeed get my paycheck on Friday.
2. I could assume the company was gone for good and start looking for a new nine-to-five.
3. Start my own business.

While working from home, I also worked on my side hustle. In the hours before my day job responsibilities, I would work on side projects for side clients. I built up enough clients on the side that it was producing about 40% of my income, but it was taking up only 20% of my time. That meant the day job took up 80% of my time to produce only 60% of my income.

My wife and I had no kids then and only a mortgage and car payment. She also had a job, so I did the math and, in the worst case scenario of a 60% loss in income on my side, we could still pay our bills. I figured that was as calculated as a risk as I was ever going to be able to take, and I chose option #3. I took the leap of faith and started SEOnational.com.

I followed my former employer's court case as the weeks and months went on. At the age of 29, he was sentenced to 32 and a half years in federal prison. From him, I learned not to be greedy.

Freeing up that 80% of day job time allowed me to dedicate more time to my small portfolio of clients, and it took me only about two months to make that lost 60% of income back.

The first year I started my business, it was just cool to be self-employed.

As I slowly continued growing, I brought on my first team member. Guess who it was? The other designer that messaged me, "Did you hear?"

I had stayed in touch with him, and he'd help do piece-rate work as work began to overflow. As things continued to grow further, it eventually made sense for he and I to move him to full-time. Thirteen years later, he's still with me.

As one year of being self-employed turned into two, I realized the opportunity I had and became more intentional about growing SEO National. Somewhere around year four, I was listening to two books that same time, *E-Myth Revisited* and *The 4-Hour Workweek*.

The 4-Hour Workweek teaches you how to look for shorter paths to success. One big takeaway from the book was asking myself, "Why do I have just a few team members? Why don't I have 10 or 20 to help me scale this?"

A few months later, I doubled the size of the team, but I took that responsibility seriously and was never in a rush to grow the company. Sure, I wanted more success, but I didn't want to screw it up. And having people dependent on you that have kids that are dependent on them just hits different.

E-Myth Revisited teaches you the benefits of building a company dependent on processes and not people. When you build a business dependent on an individual person's skills, those skills leave when that person leaves. And when you replace them, the next person may be better or worse.

But when you build your business to be dependent on processes, you can maintain quality control at scale, regardless of the person doing the work, because they're following standard operating procedures. Documenting processes sucks, but it's worth it.

I estimate that it took me two-to-three hours every other day for a year to document our processes fully. I probably went deeper than many others, but I never wanted to do it again. Besides making revisions as our processes evolved, I wanted to do it right the first time. I didn't want to half-ass it, knowing I'd have to return and fix it.

It was the best thing ever. I learned a lot of principles through that process that help me guide SEO National today.

Shortly after documenting processes, we also had our first five-figure per month contract. Not a five-figure month in revenue, this was a single client with a contract of over $10,000 per month.

Had I not documented processes before that, I wouldn't have felt morally comfortable bidding on it because I knew I would not have been able to fulfill it properly. That level of confidence was the first benefit that I immediately recognized after documenting processes. Second, we got the contract. Now I had to hire half a dozen people to help fulfill it.

Just like there's no way I could have morally bid on the contract without documented processes, logistically, I couldn't have fulfilled on it either. But with processes documented, I hired efficient team members, plugged them into our project management system, and let it rip.

Regarding what you need to succeed, the idea of documenting processes is an action. Now, let's talk about a characteristic you need to be successful.

Embrace delayed gratification.

Sure, there are many ways that you can grow a business aggressively, but most are not sustainable. Unicorn growth is not sustainable to your mental health, physical health, or company reputation. At some point, you will implode.

You know those crime scene movies where detectives are in a room with pictures pinned to the wall, and they're connecting strings from one picture to the next to connect the dots? I can connect the dots to 90% of my clients being referred from a client before them.

I've built a multi-seven-figure agency without ever spending a dollar on ads. You, too, can do this by having a good product, documented processes, and giving without expecting in return. What do I mean by the latter?

If you follow me online, you'll see that I constantly give away my secrets. I will tell anybody anything about all of our processes because my ideal customers value *time* more than *money*.

If knowledge were the secret, we'd all be gazillionaires because everything is readily available at our fingertips on our phones. Instead of knowledge, people pay for speed and implementation. In my eyes, you can't lose by giving away all the secrets because there are only three types of content consumers:

1. Those that read your content, take your advice, and run.

   Fantastic. They were never your custom anyway, so you didn't lose them. But you did help them, which will increase your reach and reputation.

2. Somebody that might need what you offer later, or they know someone that needs it.

3. The person that buys now.

You can see with these types of content consumers that you have nothing to lose by giving everything away for free, but you do have a lot to gain.

The other nice thing about constantly giving away free value is that your audience subconsciously builds a relationship with you. They begin to understand your personality and your skillset. Then, when they reach out to buy what you offer, there is very little selling involved. Nearly all of my "sales calls" are like conversations with friends. "Hi, Damon. I know you're awesome at SEO. Let's talk about that. But, first, what you shared about your wife and kids was really cool. When can we start?"

They follow you for your expertise but convert because they relate to you as a human. As you grow, remember that this is a mental marathon way more than anything else. You're an army of one. Nobody is going to save you. No one cares about your problems. Everything—good or bad—is your fault.

Setema Gali is a motivational speaker that I learned about recently. I heard him speak for the first time at Russell Bronson's Unlock the Secrets event. He had an interesting catchphrase that stuck with me:

"Define your why."

But he elaborated. Figure out your *why* for everything; your *why* for work, for family, and define it. Once you define it, "you'll be willing to crawl over broken glass for all of it."

Why that resonated with me so much is not that it motivated me, but it connected the dots for me.

- It helped me better understand my drive.
- Why I continue to succeed.
- Why others don't understand my drive.

Because I know my *why*, memories and legacy for my family, nothing will stop me from accomplishing it. Everyone should define their *why*. What is your drive?

→ Is it because you want to provide for your family?

→ Is it because you want to prove somebody wrong from your childhood?

Once you know that, you become your #1 fan. You, too, will be willing to crawl over broken glass for anything. Nobody or nothing will stop you.

Those around you will either support you and want to grow with you, or it may tear you apart. They see your drive as a mirror reflecting their insecurities as you grow, and they remain stuck.

But there is always a better version of you to be had. The you in one year can be greater than the you now. The you in five years can do things the past version of you never imagined possible.

SEOnational.com

My Gold Nugget Takeaways

Chapter 10
Hernan Vazquez

Hernan Vazquez is an entrepreneur and digital marketing expert with over 13 years of experience in creating advertising and marketing campaigns that focus on bringing clients and students more clients, leads and profit. Over the past 7 years, he's been responsible for over $60M+ in profitable social media ad spend and generated over $200M in revenue for clients. Founder of "Scale Driven" a top-tier business development agency that focuses on helping companies increase revenue by developing better digital marketing and advertising initiatives. With team members throughout the United States, South America, and Europe, his company works with clients worldwide.

Hey agency owner! My name is Hernan Vazquez, and I'm super excited to share with you what I learned after working as the marketing and media buying director at an 8-figure ad agency and after launching several 7-figure advertising agencies myself. I'll show you the do's and don'ts in growing your digital marketing agency and what separates those agency owners who enjoy every minute from those who are stressed out and burned out, because that was exactly my case.

I went from completely and totally overwhelmed building an 8-figure ad agency, to the joy of growing my own advertising agency to 7 figures (and getting it 2 Comma Club Award for it), traveling around the world extensively, focusing on what I do best and building a great team of people that makes the business better every single day. There were some mindset shifts I had to make in order to make this a reality, and I want to share them with you so you can achieve the life you want.

First, let me briefly introduce myself. I've been in digital marketing for the past 12 years and have done almost everything imaginable. I began by writing articles on Fiverr® for $4 each to pay the bills and put food on the table, which led me to my first "agency" clients. I did great work form them and over-delivered on their articles, which resulted in a handful of people reaching out privately to do some additional work for them. And boy, I'd take it.

▶ **What was the greatest mindset or identity shift you had to have to be as successful as you are?**

I have learned a LOT of things in the process of doing project for clients and myself. I have set up pages in WordPress® (I'm not a web designer), done SEO, light coding (I'm really not a programmer), social media management, designing logos and brands, email marketing, and setting up automations with Zapier® and IFTTT®, etc. I am really hands-on in everything I do, and that's the first mindset shift that I had to make. I used to think that I needed to know how to *do everything myself* before delegating it to one of my employees or VAs to do it, and that's simply not true (more on this later).

During my career, I've had the honor and privilege to work with guys like Grant Cardone, Frank Kern, Dean Graziosi, Tony Robbins, Dan Henry, Paul Getter, Patrick Bet-David, Jeff Lerner, and many others, always in some sort of "agency" capacity. Specifically, I would provide services for them, especially in the paid Facebook ads space. In some cases, my clients would even hire me as their marketing director/CMO (like Grant Cardone, Frank Kern, and Jeff Lerner did), or I would simply run their ads and help them make their funnels better. This is another thing that I learned:

Focus is key.

I went from doing everything and anything under the sun to becoming really, really good at one or two things. Currently, my agency is known worldwide as one of the top Facebook ad agencies just because of our experience and the budgets we manage for our clients. Early in my career, I learned that saying "yes" to everything will only bring trouble. I had a mentality of "saying yes or I'd lose clients," which not only brought the worst type of clients to my agency, but also saturated and overwhelmed my team.

That was until I learned to say "no," let some potential clients go, and go "tunnel-vision" on a couple of services/skill sets. I will go into more detail about this later because it impacts the quality of clients you get and how much you can charge for your services.

In 2018, I became Grant Cardone and Frank Kern's marketing and media buying director for their growing advertising agency. It was a wild ride. We went from 30 or so clients to over 250 within 8-9 months. We were just shy of 7 figures per month in revenue, and I had to train, hire and manage over 20 media buyers and take care of most of the marketing campaigns that kept the agency growing. I was also responsible for providing each of those clients with results. Every single one!

It was extremely fun and quite challenging. I learned a lot during this process, especially what to do, what not to do, and how to avoid burnout as an agency owner. In fact, after I parted ways with Grant Cardone, I decided I'd never have a marketing agency again! It just wasn't my cup of tea to run an agency that big with lots of employees and lots of stress. I'd rather be doing anything else, like coaching, info products, etc.. That was, however, until I met some people a few years later who also owned digital marketing agencies BUT they were having a blast. They traveled the world, lived their dream lives with their families, and enjoyed their lives. I began thinking, "There's got to be a better way." And there is!

In May 2021, I decided to drop everything and focus entirely on my advertising agency. I had a number of partnerships (I was part of the board of several education companies), the marketing director and consulting gigs (I was the marketing director for Jeff Lerner and Entre Institute at the time), etc. I decided to do it differently this time. I would take all I had learned (and what I'm about to show you) and apply them to my own agency. And it was one of the best decisions of my life.

For example, during the second half of 2021, I partnered with Paul Getter and James Starr, and we launched an agency servicing strictly financial advisors. It was great. Not only are Paul and James great guys, but the way we launched this from scratch was the key. We set out to hire great people and set up great processes so we could dedicate ourselves to doing what we loved the most. Once I learned that, I got my faith back in building marketing agencies that could help me achieve my dream lifestyle. Following is what I learned through the years about building a profitable, sustainable and fulfilling digital marketing agency. I hope it helps you!

▶ Learning #1: Focus As Much As Possible.

One thing that was really overwhelming in this 8-figure ad agency experience I mentioned earlier was that we'd say "yes" to any type of client. We serviced mom-and-pop shops, local businesses, webinar funnels, coaches and consultants, e-commerce stores, car dealerships, chiropractors, lawyers, personal brands, info-product companies, app businesses, high-ticket funnels and more.

We built landing pages for them, ran their Facebook and Instagram® ads, ran contextual advertising for them, advised them on their sales processes, and shared email sequences with them. We helped in any way we could.

I'm sure you can imagine the operational and fulfillment nightmare that this was, along with the impact on our team. For example, the agency media buyers could handle fewer accounts because they had to pivot their thinking every time they started working with a new client. There's a big difference in how you buy ads for a webinar funnel versus a local chiropractor that wants more walk-ins. The account managers had to make custom reports for everyone because each funnel and KPIs were different. The communication and lingo were different for each client. Some clients talked about "patients" or "units" while others talked about "booked calls."

We even designed their logos and did some therapy counseling for them (I'm just semi-kidding here, but God bless those account managers). Bottom line, we would service anyone with whatever they needed, and this was no bueno.

I decided to only offer Facebook ad services to coaches, consultants, and info-product owners. That's it. There's more than enough money, clients, and growth in this niche to build a really big agency if you want to. This focus allowed me to get some great clients that pay good money and are worth a lot to us (between $50,000 to $100,000 per client). They also stay for a long time and refer other clients too! It's great.

You see, there are two main focus factors that to consider. One is the niche factor, and the other one is the service factor. Who is going to be your main niche, and what is going to be your main service? If you had to choose only one niche and only one service to deliver and sell, what would that be?

The reason I'm so adamant about focusing is that it makes everything easier. Client attraction is easier (you become the go-to agency in your niche, and you start getting a decent number of referrals), and fulfillment is easier (your employees know your client's lingo and what's important for them, and they can use this to provide better results), reporting is easier, client management is easier, etc. It also allows you to charge more money.

Remember that the main focus of this chapter is to build an agency that enables you to live the lifestyle of your dreams, and you can't do that if you're constantly putting out fires. Focusing "an inch wide but a mile deep" makes a big difference in how your agency performs.

Sometimes my entrepreneurial ADD will kick in, and I have to restrain myself because I immediately want to go into other verticals, other traffic sources, etc.

For example, I decided to really go in with my digital agency and determined that we would offer two services "levels." We would offer an "ads only" package and a "full-funnel" package. In the first one, we would run their ads and advise on their funnel performance, take a look at the customer journey, provide templates, etc. In the second, we would do everything for them (copywriting, email sequences, design, etc.). We would become their marketing team-in-a-box. At this point you may be thinking, "Hernan, you didn't learn anything."

However, I had a "come to Jesus" moment when we did the math. I hired a team to calculate our profit per client based on how many hours the team would dedicate to each client (if you own a digital marketing agency and you're not doing this, I highly suggest you do).

The results were staggering but not surprising. Our profit margin per "ads only" client was around 60%-80%, while on the "full-funnel" clients, we were making a 40%-50% profit margin. Needless to say, we went all-in selling "ad only" packages and reserved the full funnel packages for clients we had worked with for a while, a back-end sell, or simply for those that made a lot of sense or those we could charge a lot of money. This brings us to the next lesson.

▶ **Learning #2: Charge More Money.**

I learned this during my career: Cheaper clients complain the most. It's incredible how raising prices can impact your agency, your client's quality, and your team performance.

I have always struggled with this. I grew up in a third-world country where my mom and dad always fought about money at our dinner table. That instilled in me a scarcity mentality that took a lot of years of entrepreneurship, coaching, mentorship, and successes to get in check. I still, to this day, need to remind myself of the ungodly amount of opportunity and wealth out there.

For this reason, I decided to be in Russel Brunson's' Inner Circle, and in doing so, put myself in rooms with people who had more success than me at that time. I went out to places with a lot of wealth and money moving around, just to breathe the air and soak in a new reality. For example, one of the things that I like to do when I'm in Miami is to sit at this specific Starbucks on Collins Avenue, right in the middle of Sunny Isles Beach, just to watch the car passing by. Once you see enough Rolls Royces, Lamborghinis, Bentleys, and Ferraris, you will be convinced that you can do better.

This may not be your style, but it helps me put things in perspective. Another example is a video I recently saw from Elon Musk. He was being asked what it was like to be the wealthiest person in the world.

He said that he didn't think about that a lot, but what he did think about is how every minute of high-quality thinking on his end is worth around $1 million for Tesla.

One. Million. Dollars. Per. Minute. of Elon Musk dedicating his time to "high-quality thinking." That's real scale and wealth and opportunity. That hit really me hard.

During my 8-figure ad experience, we made the mistake of pricing ourselves too low. We were the "affordable" option, so people came in just to give us a go because they didn't have much to lose. The main result of this was that several unqualified clients "made it through," became clients, and dropped after a couple weeks of not seeing results.

Here's the main problem with this: most of your teams' hours for a client, the grunt work, getting everything up to speed and the whole onboarding experience is during the first 2-4 weeks of engagement. Once a client is up and running and getting results, managing them is much easier because they trust you and are happy. So if clients drop after 30 days, you're actually losing money.

Here's another problem: There's no real difference between charging $2,000 per month for your services and $5,000 or $10,000 per month. I had a client paying me $30,000 per month for full marketing services. I've done it, and it's just a number. Of course, we need to deliver 10 times the value we're charging, but of course, we are going to do that anyway. The point is that the amount of work is basically the same.

The one thing that does change is your clients' quality. Charging more money is great because you can earn much more revenue with fewer clients and really service them. I mean we are putting *real* effort into their campaigns. We have more people working for them, give thembetter resources, etc.

When you sell yourself short, everyone loses. Your client loses because you can't service them well. Your team loses because they need to serve more clients to justify their salaries (which impacts focus and quality). You lose because you're not making enough at the end of the month.

I encourage you to make a decision, right here, right now, to increase your prices by 50% today. From now on, charge 50% more to every person you encounter and watch what happens. Once you start hearing a lot of "Yes," you increase another 50%, and so on. You will see that you can increase your revenue significantly just by doing this. I truly recommend reading *$100M Offers* by Alex Hormozi. He explains why charging more money for your services is the way to go.

▶ **Learning #3: Hire Awesome People and Empower Them To Take Over.**

I learned that there are basically 2 ways of hiring and managing people. The first one is to hire people for specific tasks, build the processes for them and give them specific instructions on how to do things based on how you (or someone else in your team) have done it before. The other way is to hire someone and give them a goal and let them take over.

In my experience, you need both in your agency. You need doers, and you need thinkers. You need *B-players*, and you need *A-players*. I never knew that A-players existed until I started talking to other agency owners that were crushing it, and they also seemed really happy about their advertising agency.

Because I'm hands-on, I would learn and do things myself first, then pass it on to my VAs/employees. Of course, this has a limit,especially if you want to build an agency that outgrows you and enables you to do whatever you want. This is especially true if you're venturing into the "unknown" world of legal, HR, growing a sales team, etc. These are things I'm not wired for, and this was another significant mindset shift that I had to make.

One of the things that made all the difference was hiring a General Manager for my agency. Her name is Mika, and she's awesome. She used to be my executive assistant, but she wanted more, so we tried it and it was one of the best decisions ever. The team loves her, and she's definitely an A-player. She handles all team communication, problem-solving, and basically, making the agency better daily.

My goal was to take the agency to 80% "there," meaning that the clients were getting results, we were acquiring and onboarding good clients every month, and things were running smoothly. After that, we empower the team to bring it to 95%. For the record, I don't think we ever get to 100% in a digital marketing agency, or any business for that matter. But getting it to 90%-95% means that every day the agency is getting better, the team is getting better, the processes are getting better, etc. Everything is a result of the commitment of the people that work there.

In order to reach the 80% mark, I needed processes, and remember, I was used to creating the processes myself. Unless you are gifted in processes and enjoy creating them, I suggest you get your employees to create your processes for you. In fact, people that are closer to doing the actual thing are the ones that should be responsible for creating the processes. This is difficult for many agency owners, especially the "doers" like me who think they need to create the processes themselves. Here's the good news: You don't. Let your B-players create the processes, and your A-players can polish them, store them, and set reminders to update them.

Here is something to consider: this is not a cheap and easy route. You will invest a lot of money and time into developing your A-players. You might lose some clients in the process, but that's part of the investment over the long run. If you want to grow your agency, or any business for that matter, you need to relinquish control. As a control freak, I can tell you that it is not an easy task.

Empower people to take over, make decisions, hit goals, and set the dashboards to have visibility. These are things that they should have also help you build. The difference between an A-player and a B-player is that an A-player will report back to you and hunt you down to get the stuff they need to do their jobs, so be prepared. In the case of B-players, you need to hunt them down to get reports, etc. Let me remind you that you need both. Ideally, your A-players will be your leaders, and your B-players will be doers.

Another thing to consider is that there needs to be some upside for your A-players for them to be invested in your agency. There are a million ways to do this, but what we decided was to designate some percentage of profits into a pool that gets distributed among the key employees every quarter.

▶ Learning #4: Step Back And Focus On What Really Matters.

Going back to the Elon Musk example, imagine if Elon would focus on things that don't matter as much or if he would focus on the wrong things. That would have an immense (and catastrophic) impact on his businesses. The same goes for anyone using a lot of leverage to grow their businesses. I heard once that Jeff Bezos' main goal was to make one decision per quarter. And that's it. If you think about it, that's a billion dollar decision he needs to make, so it makes sense he only makes a handful of decisions per year.

I decided that, over the long run, I would only focus on three things: Vision, Growth, and Marketing. I enjoy marketing so much, I really do. I log into my Facebook ads dashboard daily, tweak and launch the ads, write copy, create landing pages, and launch email sequences to our list. I fully intend to keep doing it because I really enjoy it. I also enjoy helping other entrepreneurs by creating content, and coaching our students. At some point I will likely hire a marketing intern or assistant to help me with my ideas and eventually have a marketing team for our brand, but I would still be involved in some capacity.

I also enjoy taking sales calls from time to time. Networking with awesome people and growth is part of what I am and what I do. I want to keep focusing on that and finding new ways, verticals, products, and offers we can launch, at least for now.

This is important: when it comes to vision, no one can do it for me. I ask myself, "What are the one or two things that nobody else can do except me?" and then I only do that. Of course, I still get caught in the weeds from time to time, dealing with client issues and client meetings, but this is something I am empowering my team to take over. All in all, I dedicate one to two hours per week to anything that is outside these 3 core pillars.

This is something I learned after working with some big dogs. They only focus on what they're extremely good at and hire people to do the rest. For example, once I was with Frank Kern in his office, and we were scheming a campaign to launch a new product. I saw him writing an ad and landing page, live, on the spot. It was like magic. I felt like I was witnessing a miracle, like Lebron James playing a game or Lionel Messi with a free kick (for my soccer fans out there). And that hit me hard.

I encourage you to ask yourself, "What are things that I'm extremely good at, and I want to keep betting on?" This way, you can become part of the .01%, and hire A-players to help you with the rest.

I hope this is helpful and that you enjoyed this chapter. I have nothing to sell you, but feel free to subscribe to our podcast at **ScaleDriven.com/listen** or find me (Hernan Vazquez) on Youtube®.

See you soon!

My Gold Nugget Takeaways

Chapter 11
Karen Sahetya

Karen Sahetya, coach to agency owners inside the Agency Think Tank and agency owner, has established herself and her team among the internet's leading marketers.

In an online world where noise of the newest online trends can drown out practical experience, Karen has inspired and led thousands of agency owners through the most essential strategies and processes they need to build and scale profitable agencies.

With nearly a decade of corporate marketing experience with Fortune 500 companies plus over a decade of agency ownership, Karen combines the best in offline marketing systems and processes with expertise in digital marketing to help agencies get off the revenue rollercoaster and stop the client churn cycle.

▶ **What was the greatest piece of advice you received from a mentor or coach that made the biggest impact in your agency journey?**

I've received a lot of great (and some not so great) advice along my journey. When I first decided to leave corporate in the rearview mirror and take the leap into entrepreneurship, I sought the wisdom of someone who had more experience running a company than anyone I knew.

Mr. Holland was the CEO of the company I'd essentially grown up in as a young professional. He's the kind of leader who doesn't have to be the loudest voice in the room. He leads from a place of respect, quiet strength, and thoughtfulness.

Over lunch one day, he was kind enough to listen to all my ideas, big plans, and eager dreams. He shared with me some insights he observed from the current market, economic trends, and the impact they would have for businesses. I was in awe of the way he observed and processed information, not to mention the knowledge he had gained in his decades of leading a company. So when I asked what advice he could give me as I embarked on my own entrepreneurial journey, I prepared myself for the hidden economic trend or tidbit of knowledge that I might've missed in business school.

Instead, he told me to make getting a great executive assistant my first priority.

Hire somebody? I didn't even have a client yet and definitely didn't have any revenue. I nodded with humility and knew that even if I didn't understand why that was the one piece of advice he felt was most important to give me, I should keep it top of mind.

I flashed back to several years before that moment to my college advisor and business professor telling me that even if I didn't learn a single thing from her classes, to remember to get a good lawyer and a good CPA. Of all the things she shared with us, why would it be most important for us to remember to hire a good lawyer and good CPA? I didn't have a business at the time, didn't know what kind of business I might ever have, but she was fast-forwarding to hiring these two roles.

In case you're wondering, I listened to both of them. When I launched my business, before I had my first client or any money to worry about managing, I interviewed attorneys across the country including some from the biggest and most renowned law firms. I wanted to work with some of the most powerful companies in the world and I wanted to make sure I showed up ready to play. I hired the attorney I still work with today and knew that while I might not fully know why I hired the best, I could check this one off my list. I did the same thing in hiring a CPA and my next order of business was to actually get some business.

Once the revenue started flowing and the clients started multiplying, Mr. Holland's words echoed in my ears and I realized I needed help. I didn't have a clearly defined job description and I made every mistake in the book during the hiring process, nevertheless hired my first assistant for the business. When she asked me what she'd be doing, I literally said she could do anything she wanted because I needed help with everything. Thankfully she took the job, saw me through many chapters of the business, and became someone I still hold dear to me.

It was only after many more hires and years later that it finally clicked for me. Both of these mentors had the experience and the foresight to focus on building a team and they were essentially giving me the same advice: hire good people and don't try to do it all yourself. The impact you want to create whether for your own family or for the masses comes with scale, and scale requires you to build a team.

If you try to do it all yourself, you'll burn out long before you've had a chance to make the impact you want. Take the time to find the right people for the right positions and then let them do what they do best. Your time should be spent doing the things that only you can do, which is a lot shorter of a list than you might think. If you let your time get consumed, then the things your business needs most to survive—your leadership, vision, and strategy—all by the wayside.

▶ **What would you say was the biggest contributing factor to your success?**

Mindset is at the core of everything we do. After a few ups and downs personally and in business, I was inspired by a mentor to track my revenue alongside the highs and lows of my mindset. I started rating every day and matching it up to the revenue into the business for that day. Sure enough, the peaks and valleys of my revenue and mindset aligned for a clear visualization of how my mindset inspired or dragged down the momentum.

It's hard to sell to people when you're not sold on yourself. It's hard to show up for people if you're not showing up for yourself. It's hard to deliver for people if you're not delivering for yourself. It all starts with you and your ability to protect your mindset.

For me, an abundance mindset has been a huge contributor to the success of my business. I truly believe that the prospects or clients I speak with have so much opportunity, and I believe the same for myself and my team.

When fear and money scarcity starts to creep in, it's difficult to ask prospects to invest in you because you're not ready to invest in yourself. In this headspace, instead of providing a service that propels your clients to the next level, you begin to take on their problems.

What happens when a prospect who doesn't have the funds to invest in your service approaches you? If you are coming from a place of scarcity about leads or money, in order to close the deal you lower your prices. In turn, you find yourself short on the money to invest in yourself and your team. Instead of showing them the path to success, you quite literally have taken on their lack of funds and made it your own.

I've coached thousands of freelancers and agency owners by troubleshooting their client campaigns, giving them our exact systems and processes, and sharing everything my team and I have built into my own agency. At all levels of agency ownership, I've seen abundance mindsets slip away and scarcity start to creep in. Nobody is immune to it for eternity, even if you naturally have more of an abundance mindset.

There are always circumstances that can shake your core, but if you have clarity about how much opportunity truly exists and the role you can play in your own success, you can keep those feelings of scarcity from creeping in and spiraling you down a different path.

Every once in a while, an agency owner will ask me why I would be willing to train my competition, and the answer is because I have an abundance mindset. I see us as collaborators, partners in this crazy entrepreneurial game, and I want them to succeed.

I know that there's opportunity everywhere and that inspires me to work in a way that leaves people better than I found them. Sometimes that means referring a prospect to an agency who is a better fit, even if the prospect is ready to pay me. Other times that means helping a team member step into a role with another business that can offer them an opportunity better aligned with their interests.

This approach frees me of any distraction about competition, allows me to align myself with people who would otherwise be seen as competitors, and fosters a more transparent and generous relationship with prospects, clients, team, and other agencies.

▶ **What is the greatest skill you needed to develop to be as successful as you are?**

The greatest skill that's been absolutely critical to develop has nothing to do with what we offer as an agency. It wasn't mastering Facebook (now Meta®) ads, copywriting, funnel building, business analytics, or any other technical skill. Although those skill sets are important as a solopreneur in the early days of building an agency, eventually you hit a wall and you have to give yourself a promotion, remove yourself from that technical position, and begin building a team.

Building a team is an entirely different skill set than hiring a team. It involves far more than hiring, training, and onboarding team members. It requires ongoing mentorship and leadership, and it also requires you to stop being the player and start being the coach. It's always easier to do the thing rather than coach the thing or build a process around it. But if you're unwilling to take yourself out of the game and start coaching, your success will be limited to what you can do by yourself.

Coaching is about leading people through a transformation and so is building a team for your own business. Putting in the effort to develop your team and providing an environment where they can reach their personal goals creates a culture of empowerment, autonomy, and initiative so that you can remove yourself from the day to day.

It may seem impossible at first to transfer skills that you've learned to do naturally. You may not even be fully aware of your processes to make a decision or troubleshoot a problem because it happens so quickly and effortlessly. Even where it seems intuitive and without any hint of process, take the time to dig deeper and understand all of the tiny inputs that lead you towards a specific decision or action. If you can break down those inputs, you can build a line of questioning that leads your team to discover the same solution you would provide in a given scenario. With enough practice and repetition, it will become second nature to your team as well.

Does this take tons of time you don't have? Of course it does, but here's what you really don't have time to do: you don't have time to be the sole problem solver in your business from now until eternity. Equipping your team to take ownership of problem-solving will be a gamechanger.

Along the way, especially in times of high stress, it's easy to dip back into 'doing' instead of coaching. Don't fall into this trap, and if you find yourself 'doing' again, correct your course as soon as possible. Coaches prepare the team, build game strategy, and develop players. When a sports team is headed into the second half of the game after a rough first half, you don't see the coach jump into the game and start playing on behalf of the players. A good coach breaks down what's not working, identifies strengths, leverages the right players, and inspires the team to victory. They never take the floor and start "doing" in place of their players.

So the next time you feel like taking over, instead take a seat and start coaching. If you feel like your technical skills are rusty, remember that those aren't the primary skills you need anymore. Remember that now you're the coach, not the player.

▶ **What was the greatest mindset or identity shift you had to have to be as successful as you are?**

When our leadership team came together to identify our values as an agency, it was relatively easy because we had enough similarities that our core values just spilled out of us as follows:

Radical honesty - We communicate with radical honesty to benefit our team and our clients. Our communication is transparent, yet respectful.

Integrity without exception - We operate with full integrity at all times. We tell clients when their expectations aren't realistic and we only take on those we can help.

Solutions-oriented - We are problem-solvers and we are relentless in our pursuit of solutions. No problem is a match for our creativity.

Perseverance - We persevere through the hard times with true grit and stick-to-it-tiveness. We're driven to excel and good isn't good enough.

Extreme ownership - We take responsibility beyond expectation to deliver the best possible results.

Humility - We're humble and work with confidence, but without ego so that we can continue to improve.

Constant personal growth - We have an insatiable appetite for personal growth and we're constantly looking for opportunities to learn and grow in the smallest and biggest of ways.

These values were consistent with how I was driven to deliver for clients and as we grew the team, we articulated these values so that we could hire and mentor accordingly.

By this time we'd solidified a hiring process that gave us some of the best team members we'd ever had. They were in total alignment with our values and proved it every single day. I was able to remove myself from much of the day to day with clients because they enjoyed working with the rest of the team. In fact, it didn't take long for me to see that when I hired the right person, that person was far better than me at their role.

As we continued to scale the agency, efficiency became the name of the game. We were constantly implementing processes to improve our results and efficiency. As we measured, then improved, measured, and then improved, I started to notice our output drop.

I couldn't understand it because I knew without a doubt that our team was bringing their best every day. The results were solid, but it was taking a long time to get things done and I'd find team members doing and re-doing their own work, getting caught in a vicious cycle of improving what they'd already done. Occasionally I'd find them at a standstill, unable to actually complete a task because they were only willing to do it if it was the absolute best they could do.

Every morning we had our daily meeting, we read our values aloud, knocked out some critical issues, and set the tone for the day. I began digging a little deeper, working with team members to understand where we were losing productivity, and why we were getting stuck on simple tasks, until one day, we were reading our values out loud in our morning meeting and it hit me.

Perseverance - We persevere through the hard times with true grit and stick-to-it-tiveness. We're driven to excel and **good isn't good enough**.

Team members were overcomplicating simple tasks because if good wasn't good enough, they had to work on it until it was good enough and it felt like it would never be good enough. Thirty-minute projects were taking a full day, and sometimes not getting completed at all because it's hard to start something if you believe it'll never be good enough.

I spoke to a couple of team members to get some more insight about what their obstacles were and to try and understand how our values were playing out in their minds and in their work. I was raised in an environment where constructive criticism was welcome and there was focus on constant improvement, so I couldn't inherently understand the problem. For me, every word of this value was rooted in the way I was raised.

Thanks to our radically transparent culture and the team's willingness to be open with me, I learned that to someone with a different upbringing or without context, parts of this value did a lot more harm than good.

This well-intended value created massive amounts of tension and feelings of inadequacy for brilliant team members. Once I realized this, I had to do something about it. In our next daily meeting, I announced that good IS good enough and that we were revising our values to reflect that.

We talked about the value of simplicity, how to identify the real goal (it's rarely ever to perfect something), how the work they were all capable of is more than enough, and how they individually are all more than enough. The relief on the call was palpable.

As I had said the words "it doesn't have to be perfect" out loud on the call, I realized that I truly had been expecting perfection, and chasing perfection led to constant disappointment for everyone involved. Immediately after the meeting, one by one team members reached out to me to let me know how important this seemingly small change was to them. They had been beating themselves up for months trying to make sure their work was good enough and it was weighing on them.

Changing this value required much more than editing a few words in a slide deck. With this change in values, I had to learn a new level of patience, something that wasn't naturally ingrained in me. Impatience and perfection had always served me well in business because it drove me to deliver results fast, take quick action on things that would grow the business, and be highly communicative.

But as they say, *what gets you here won't get you there.* Building a team showed me that letting go of perfection and exercising patience was one of the most important qualities I could learn as a leader. Being patient with my team even when they aren't patient with themselves has been critical to their ability to trust me as a leader, but also to trust themselves as the experts they are.

Aside from shifting identity from being the player to being the coach in the business, the biggest shift in my mindset was from always believing something could be better to believing that good is good enough.

If you're building a team, be intentional about how patient you are with others and don't forget to be patient with yourself. Patience toward yourself is grace, and to succeed you have to have plenty of it for yourself. Create your values with intention and consider how they might be perceived by your team. And remember, good is good enough. You are good enough.

For free resources on how to scale your agency up without burning out, visit **https://agencythinktank.com** and check out the Free Training Content Hub.

My Gold Nugget Takeaways

Chapter 12
Mia Paulus

Hi, I'm Mia Paulus: wife, mother of 7, CEO, and a long-time entrepreneur who has made it my life's work to serve entrepreneurs and executives, helping them rediscover their passion and live their true life purpose.

My devotion, from the very beginning, has been to simplify the process of scaling and sustaining a business for busy entrepreneurs and executives. I believe that entrepreneurs can make an incredible impact on the world and a purposeful focus is critical to meet their business objectives and visions.

As the Founder and Chief Visionary at The Centr, I get a chance to support all businesses, from startups to Fortune 500 clients in areas of marketing, sales, customer experience, employee experience, technology and accounting.

When companies have one outsourced partner to fulfill and strategize the 80% that is the same in every business, they can then focus on the 20% that makes their business unique, improving innovation and increasing their competitive advantage.

I'm one of those crazy visionary entrepreneurs. The vision I had for my agency, The Centr, was very clear 15 years ago. Despite this clarity, things didn't go as planned.

So what do I do? I have an agency done-for-you (DFY) outsourcing model I call Teamsourcing where we take on the 80% that is the same in every business giving entrepreneurs the ability to hyperfocus on the 20% that makes them unique. It's your own full-scaled operations with all the departments you need but you only have to pay for WHAT you need—WHEN you need it. That means you only pay a fractional amount for access to full-scale talent and systems. This means that ANY business of ANY size in ANY industry can benefit!

My solution for entrepreneurs is broad on purpose. Because we are broad we can build full systems, programs and projects that are not capable with niched solutions. That is how we differentiate ourselves but it has also been a challenge to build and develop.

In my 15 years of entrepreneurship I have tried everything the wrong way until I figured out the right way. Don't worry, I won't recommend you use this same technique as you can learn from the mistakes of others…hopefully me. I'm here to tell you that there is a roadmap to success and that is what I hope to share with you in this chapter.

▶ **What was the greatest piece of advice you received from a mentor or coach that made the biggest impact in your agency journey?**

One of my greatest pieces of advice I received is ironically the same advice I give most entrepreneurs I work with. The advice came from my current business coach Bart Miller right when I needed it. Sometimes the best advice is not earth shattering…we just need to be told, AGAIN, what we already know. Ready for it? "Mia, if you can stay entirely focused on just this one business…you have a billion-dollar idea."

You see, the thing is, I've been doing my current business for fifteen years and like most of us as entrepreneurs we see shiny objects, new ideas, new things and we get excited. I've been sitting on my hands for 15 years resisting and saying "no" to a lot of opportunities that have come my way. And I was getting tired. How many times have we all been told to focus? Elon Musk sums up the impact of focus beautifully, "Innovation often doesn't come through one breakthrough idea, but through a relentless focus on continuous improvement." But by taking this one piece of advice from my business coach and going "all-in," here's where I'm at.

I was determined to find a way to give entrepreneurs a roadmap, a blueprint to show them what they needed to spend their resources (time, money and energy) on based on where they were at in their business journey. I didn't want entrepreneurs to make the mistakes I've made over these last 15 years or make the same mistakes I've seen the thousands of entrepreneurs I've worked with make. We can learn from each other as entrepreneurs.

I love to find patterns and see if they are universal truths and principles. The result of finding these patterns? It's something I call **The Impact Equation**. What I was never really taught is that business advice is not "general" in nature, meaning that all advice isn't created equal for all stages of business. So I created The Impact Equation that better details out what businesses should focus on...when.

In The Impact Equation, I talk about 6 phases of business. *Ideation, Validation, Pre-Scale, Scale, Creative Expansion, and Transition*. Each phase has different areas of focus. What I realized in business is that we usually are focused but are we focused on the right things?

Here is some practical advice on focus is if you are in the early stages of business: focus on one core product, one customer profile and one market and channel of growth. We often want to go too broad too early. The more niched you can be in what you do, who you target, and how you market yourself, the faster you will grow. As you start to scale your core product in the Scale Phase you can start to expand in other channels of growth and as you move into the Creative Expansion Phase you can THEN diversify into product expansion or other products.

On my website, you can take the free Impact Equation quiz and download my Free Impact Equation PDF to see what you should focus on at your phase of business.

▶ **What would you say was the biggest contributing factor to your success?**

Before I can tell you the biggest contributing factor to my success, it's important to define what *success* means to me.

Many of us today have pivoted to wanting to become lifestyle entrepreneurs that can work from anywhere at any time. But have most of us really gotten there? Because I work with hundreds of entrepreneurs, I can confidently say—no.

Back in 2006, when I first started my business, what people viewed as success was a sellable business with a big office and a lot of employees. Nowadays working from anywhere can be viewed as a success. The problem with that is, that many of us entrepreneurs are just employees to ourselves. We are bound to our business. So I'm challenging the status quo by blending the old and the new definitions of success.

What I consider success is being a true lifestyle entrepreneur. To be specific, it is one that creates a profitable business that can run and scale without them, that is wealth building in nature. It is not just a short-lived cash flow business, but one that is sustainable, scalable and replicable that is sellable in nature and has value if you are there as the owner or not. I can honestly say that I have a team now that could run and scale my company without me.

But how do we get that kind of success? We've created a culture of instant gratification and we want it now. We have to be willing to put in the time. So how do we keep the passion alive through all the ups and downs of business? The biggest contributing factor to my success is that I have a sure foundation within my company. A foundation rooted on knowing why we do what we do, what we stand for, and the impact we plan to make through our vision.

When I got remarried, I didn't have to work for financial reasons and at the time my business was losing money. It was the perfect set-up to put being an entrepreneur aside and focus on being the full-time mom I had always longed to be. In a lot of ways it seemed like it would be so much easier, rather than trying to balance having a large family, being a CEO, running a business, etc. I spent some time praying about it and received clear direction from God. I realized there was a reason for this company and that it was a calling. So at that point, I stopped asking to be released and realized that this business was my purpose. I knew then that my business was something the world needed and was ready for.

I have been through hard trials with my business over the years. If I wasn't firmly rooted in my sure foundation I wouldn't have lasted. Understanding the foundational elements of purpose, value and vision are so important because it allows you to shift and change while still moving in the same direction. Entrepreneurship is not a straight line; it winds a lot at times but you still get there.

Today I have a great company culture and my passion and drive is as strong if not stronger than the day I started my business. Again, the key is knowing your purpose, values and vision–but I would be lying if I didn't say that my belief in God was a big part of how I handle adversity as well. I don't think I can answer this question without pointing to God and having what I call "grit and grace." So I take action and do the things I need to do by working hard (grit) while also knowing that the adversity I face will only last so long. I have seen and experienced miracles (grace) that make-up the difference which I attribute to God.

I knew these foundational principles were the only way to create a culture and environment that would inspire and empower a team to get behind a vision, create a loyal customer following, and give companies a chance to contribute more to the world. If entrepreneurs and executives desire freedom in their businesses and want a way to leverage their time, knowing why they are in business would be a necessary first step.

As agencies we will have employees. With employees come responsibilities. I put a lot of pressure on us as employers to do the right thing despite the consequences. What's right is too subjective; that is why foundational statements are so important.

In order to feel confident in decisions, to have courage over fear, to venture into the unknown, we have to be confident and unwavering in why we do what we do, what principles guide us, and where we plan to go. We first have to have a solid foundation. Each foundation will be unique based on the vision you have for your company.

Some practical advice on how to build a Purpose Statement is to write: "Why you started or do what you do + HOW that serves others"

A simple purpose statement format I like to use is:

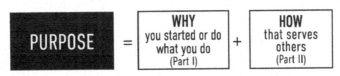

The use of values within an organization has to be intentional. They have to be interwoven in every decision whether around the customer experience (marketing, sales, service and support), employee experience (training, employee engagement and recognition, human resources), strategic partnership experience (vendor management, joint ventures, strategic alliances), or any other function that supports these three elements of the human experience in business.

A company may be able to replicate what you do or even how you do it but they will never be able to replicate your culture and why you do it. The individuals that make up your organization cannot be replicated. Never forget that organizations are only made up of people. The more you can understand the needs and wants of the people, both internal and external, the better you will be able to serve them through the identity of your purpose, values, and vision in the future.

WHY YOU NEED VALUES

1. To aid those within your organization in decision making
2. To create your desired culture and community
3. To attract your ideal customers, employees, and partners
4. To set standards for strategies and goals
5. To simplify and improve the human experience

Values should be very short—two to five words—or one word if it's a verb. Create only three to five values as they need to be easy to remember. They need to be actionable statements or words and should be philosophies, principles or beliefs that create change for good.

If you want to know how to find or refine your own individual purpose as well as the purpose, values, and vision for your company you can get a copy of my books and workbook for free, Purposeful Focus in Business at **TheCentr.com/FreeBook** to guide you.

▶ **What is the greatest skill you needed to develop to be as successful as you are?**

When I first became an "Outsourcing Expert" I was concerned because I didn't have the credentials, experience or certifications of "mainstream" methods. I didn't hyper focus on what everyone else was doing. I just wanted to solve entrepreneurs' problems in the most sustainable, scalable and replicable way possible. If I had to narrow down my "success" to one factor it would be being able and willing to connect my mind and my heart to have better discernment in the advice I receive from others. This discernment improved my ability to solve and navigate problems that are sure to arise in business.

In today's world we see two extremes: all logic or all emotion. But, to really get to the truth of business, we have to be willing to connect our heart and mind together to make decisions. You see, we are bombarded by advice from experts. Many entrepreneurs are waiting for someone to tell them what to do and many are diverted onto paths that aren't right for their business. We rely so heavily on "experts" to tell us what to think and do and a lot of times we aren't learning how to make decisions on our own. Experts tell us what systems to create and how to run our businesses. While it is valuable to have outside advice, we still want to put it through the filter of our own mind and heart, which we don't do often enough. It allows us to really process and determine what it is that we need to change.

Changing, adapting and becoming better is such a necessary part of entrepreneurship; it is what fuels our growth.

I have a unicorn brain—like many entrepreneurs. Only 1-3% of the population can do what we can do. And of course, we are all 100% unique. In short—we are rare. I have the ability to create a big vision but I also have the ability to "see it all" at a granular level. I can be very logical, systems driven, detail oriented and analytic, but also creative, innovative and fluid. This has been a blessing and a curse in my 15-year entrepreneurial journey.

It took me a long time to relinquish control. The biggest change came when I intentionally let the balls drop in my business. I had to be "okay" with customers not being happy for a while. But when I did this, something magical happened. My team picked up the balls I had dropped! When your employees are in the right seats on the bus and are empowered, you realize they can be 1000% better at their job than you ever could be.

Once I let go it freed up my time and energy to focus on my vision and the direction I wanted my company to go. I can travel for business, participate in masterminds, go on vacations, etc., all because I know that the operations and client fulfillment for my company is taken care of by an awesome team. It has come full circle. What I hoped to accomplish by simplifying business for *entrepreneurs* I had fulfilled for *me*. Do I still work a lot? Yes, but not because I have to. I love to create and execute on my vision.

With organizations first having a foundation built upon their purpose, values, and vision, decisions will now be able to be made with the heart and mind connected. They will be able to see all perspectives to make the best possible decisions. *Financial* is just one factor of many when making decisions. Which factor has the most weight will be determined by each company's unique situation. However, the decision should never compromise or challenge purpose, values, and vision. These are the foundational attributes that companies should stand for despite outward and inward pressures.

As a result, within organizations, we can start to see people, not numbers. I know the minute I start to treat my business strictly based on numbers, I will lose sight of seeing the hearts of people. Making decisions strictly on quota whether revenue, race, religion, gender, or creed will only lead to more segregation. Now I'm not saying we don't run our businesses for profits. I'm not saying we don't seek out those that need our help. More profits allow for greater contribution and impact. More lives lifted lead to a better world. Freedom and agency of individuals, and being true to our purpose, values, and vision of our company outshines making decisions based on outward appearance and pressure.

The goal of this chapter as you are building your agency is to show you the deeper side of business and to encourage others to create more "real" companies with less facades. When we do the right thing and take action, no matter the consequences, grace or luck—whatever we choose to call it—will follow. Happiness and the abundant life ripples to others.

The book, *4 Disciplines of Execution* by Chris McChesney, Jim Huling, and Sean Covey greatly influenced me, how my company sets goals, and how we view revenue and money. This book introduced me to the concept of lag and lead measurements in business.

After learning about these two data points, goal setting and how we as people can directly influence results became very clear.

Money or revenue is a *lagging indicator* in business.

It is something that occurs after or as a result of doing something else. A *leading indicator*, by comparison, is an action that can directly influence the lagging indicator, or in this case money. I know businesses need money to survive and thrive, but focusing only on money will not drive results or create happiness in our business and life.

In comparison, the more we can improve the experience for our customers, employees, and partners (leading indicators), success will follow. Money is a result of those actions. The company that best serves their market will be the leader in their market. That is true innovation. Money becomes a result of this innovative philosophy. Money can then be used as a tool to contribute and impact the world on a greater scale.

We will continue to be disappointed if money is solely our focus. The old saying, "money doesn't buy happiness" still rings true today. The key to happiness and lifelong success and significance is purposeful focus, which is the intention of this chapter. As Tony Robbins says, "Where focus goes, energy flows."

These foundations resources can help be a guide to you as you are navigating through the conflicting advice you hear from experts. When you learn how to use your mind and heart together, you'll be able to discern what you should do next both now and in the future.

▶ **What was the greatest mindset or identity shift you had to have to be as successful as you are?**

I paid $50,000 to be a part of Russell Brunson's Inner Circle. The ONE thing that has made this investment worth it literally had nothing to even do with what Russell offered as part of his Inner Circle. It had EVERYTHING to do with who was in that room.

The requirement to be a part of this group is $1 million in revenue per year or higher so by just being a part of the group they don't question your ability or grit. The result of them believing in me? A stronger

BELIEF in myself. My greatest identity shift was around belief. It's odd that 15 years later in business I still have to fight belief–or rather lack of belief. When you surround yourself with people that believe in you then you can turn to them when things get tough or when you need to talk something out. You can trust that they have your best interest at heart and the motivation to help you be what you want to be, what you were meant to be.

The thing is at each phase of business and with every new height comes new territory. With new territory comes a new level of belief. My advice would be the sooner we start associating with those at and above our same level in business the sooner you will see success. The sooner we can get rid of the toxic people around us pulling us down the more enjoyable our path to success will be. Sometimes those that hold us back can be our family or even just the employees that are "comfortable" with the stage of business we are in. Remember, not everyone is ready for your vision. It's incredible how much momentum we can achieve when we just get better at discerning who the right people are to talk with about our vision.

Even if I got nothing else out of the Inner Circle other than belief it would be worth it. I also paid $40,000 a year for my business coach. You know the biggest benefit I get from him? He has undeniable belief in me. These people I associate with elevate me to higher heights. My advice to you? Start associating with people that believe in you and are further along than you as soon as possible. It sounds so simple but it's life-changing. If you don't already have one, find a trusted advisor that guides you based on principles. Having that support system while also being rooted in your sure foundation will get you through the hard times.

Belief in yourself and your vision is a requirement for success. You will only be as big as the belief in yourself. If you have big dreams, hang out with people that also have big dreams and are further along than you are in business. They will not question your ability because you are in the same room as them.

Entrepreneurship is about taking risks. You aren't always going to know the pathway forward. Sometimes you have to take a step and hope there is something to stand on. But if you connect your mind and heart and have a sure foundation to help discern through all the noise and advice then you can make quality decisions. Of course data is important and you should make educated decisions but there are times that, even with all the data, there still won't be a clear answer on which way to go. Sometimes those decisions will be leaps of faith. In those times you have to choose and move forward full steam ahead which is where the risk and the faith come into play. Then if something along the way makes you shift directions then you do that.

That is the essence of entrepreneurship: you take steps off the ledge, you keep going, you shift, you pivot, you problem solve and you keep doing that over and over.

When you accept that business is difficult (and life is difficult) then it doesn't seem as difficult any more. You learn to just solve problems as they come. You put one foot in front of the other and take it a day at a time while also keeping a pulse on your long term direction.

Ultimately, entrepreneurship is not for everyone. But if you are committed to it and you feel called to be an entrepreneur don't do it alone, have a team and a support system that believes in you and your vision. One of my favorite quotes to reiterate this point is from, The Road Less Traveled by M. Scott Peck, M.D.,

> "Life is difficult. This is a great truth, one of the greatest truths. It is a great truth because once we truly see this truth, we transcend it. Once we truly know that life is difficult— once we truly understand and accept it—then life is no longer difficult. Because once it is accepted, the fact that life is difficult no longer matters."

Business isn't for the faint of heart but it is so amazing to see the innovation and creativity that can come from business. It's going to be hard, you're going to hit roadblocks and you might wonder if it's worth it.

Agency models involve people. Lots of them. With team building comes responsibility. That is why for this chapter I have chosen to focus on the foundational elements and mindset of business. Without them I wouldn't be where I am today. I would have lost that spark long ago. Agency models solve a lot of problems. Today people want time more than anything else. With Done-For-You services we are able to simplify business and ultimately the life of others. We are needed and we believe that.

But remember…

It's the journey of becoming that is the most valuable not the final destination. So remember to enjoy the process along the way to your awesome agency success!

Additional Resources:

You can take the free Impact Equation quiz and download my Free Impact Equation PDF to see what you should focus on at your phase of business on my website.

If you want to know how to find or refine your own individual purpose as well as the purpose, values, and vision for your company you can get a copy of my books and workbook for free, *Purposeful Focus in Business* at **TheCentr.com/FreeBook**.

My Gold Nugget Takeaways

The Owners

Chapter 13
Dawn Sinkule

Hi I'm Dawn Sinkule. I am an MBA graduate with over 17 years of experience at a Fortune 25 retail company. During my time in corporate America, I successfully managed billion-dollar budgets and led teams of thousands. I have since successfully created, managed, and operated an award-winning, unique boutique agency: Digital Dawn.

Digital Dawn is an ideal marketing partner for million-dollar e-commerce brands that need targeted expertise to catapult their business to next-level profitability. Digital Dawn has been in business for more than 8 years and has helped hundreds of eCommerce brands plan, grow and profit online.

The award-winning Digital Dawn team of cream-of-the-crop professionals specializes in marketing and financial consulting, paid media, conversion rate optimization, email marketing, design, and more. My team is committed to strategically guiding and supporting eComm entrepreneurs toward expanding their growth and increasing profitability. Digital Dawn's 6-step D2D methodology is a proven hands-on, personalized approach that ensures business owners won't lose sleep over where ad spend is going or whether they have the inventory to make it through a launch. Every service Digital Dawn provides is data-driven and customized to meet unique business needs so owners can be confident their business is on the right track to your desired results.

▶ **What was the greatest piece of advice you received from a mentor or coach that made the biggest impact in your agency journey?**

I've had a lot of mentorships over the years ranging from paid high powered professionals in a corporate setting, to mentors in mastermind groups, to professional development groups. But the reality is that the best advice that was given to me was given from people in my family. I know it might sound a little cheesy, but they are the people who are closest to me, the ones who see me every day, know the struggle and can see the passion and purpose behind what I'm trying to do.

I remember one night at a family dinner I was telling my family that I was nervous to put out a big proposal to a potential client. I was dealing with all the imposter syndrome feelings: "What if I'm not as good as the other agencies? What happens if I'm priced too high or too low? What if I can't deliver?" It was the string of all the things we as agency owners think (or at least I do), and I remember my daughter said to me, "You're the best mom! How can nobody like what you do? Don't be scared, you have to try." And then my husband said, "Yeah, what happens if you don't try? Think how much they will be missing out on your brilliance." And finally, my son said, "Mom, everybody likes you." WOW! Just a little bit of cheerleading and confidence from those closest really made an impact in my ability to see if I didn't put things out in the world, how would I even know if they would work? If they actually did work I would make an impact, so it's my duty to put myself out there.

One of my favorite quotes and one that I live by even to this day is this:

> "There is freedom waiting for you,
> On the breezes of the sky,
> And you ask 'What if I fall?'
> Oh but my darling,
> What if you fly?"
> ~by Erin Hanson

One of my favorite quotes and personal mottos that I'm teaching my children, my team and my clients is this: We are all scared at first, but the world needs our gifts and if we don't put them out there, then someone else might not get the benefit of our skills.

▶ **What would you say was the biggest contributing factor to your success?**

Success is a strange thing, and after coming from a corporate background I had high hopes for what "success" was going to look like for me. What I can tell you is that success looks different for everyone. For me, success was about being able to be my own boss, not having to work for or with anyone again that I didn't like, having the time and freedom to be with my family, enjoying what I do, AND, of course, making money doing it. Because of course if you're not actually getting paid for what you're doing, then it's really just a hobby.

For me and the success of my agency, it has come down to being really clear on who we serve. This has changed over the years as I've learned more and more about what and who I like to work with, but practically speaking, you can't work with everyone. You have to get specific on who you want to serve.

Secondly, I would say that being clear on what you *don't* offer is just as important as what you *do* offer. At the beginning of the agency, I was doing anything and everything for anyone. This made it virtually impossible to scale, hard to hire and I couldn't make anything repeatable because we were doing so many different things.

You know the saying "the riches are in the niches?" Well, this is true to a degree. I think the niches might change the longer you stay in business, the more you learn your strengths and the more you work with different businesses, but for the most part, getting clear on who I wanted to work with and what I wanted to offer made everything so much easier. From marketing to sales pitches, knowing what we did and didn't do and who we did it with.....once I got clear and comfortable with that AND with saying no to those who didn't meet my expectations or fall into that category. From then on, the more stable and scalable things became.

Clarity, clarity, clarity equals scalability.

▶ **What is the greatest skill you needed to develop to be as successful as you are?**

One of the most crucial skills for achieving success doesn't really have anything to do with education or all the thousands of dollars I've spent on courses, programs, masterminds etc. It has to do with a few simple, but oh so hard skills.

The first is drive. You have to want to get up every morning, work hard and move the needle forward. For me, I get up every morning just like

I'm going to a "job," get dressed, go to my "office" and set myself up for the day. I have a start time, a lunch time, a break time and an end of the day. It helps keep me on track, and you might think, "Well geez, I'm doing this so I don't have to have the sort of rigidness." And that's fine, but for me, having the structure and the routine helps me stay motivated and keeps me focused on the fact that this isn't a hobby, this is my life now and if I want to be successful I have to treat it like a successful business. Even when I first started with the agency, and even when I wasn't exactly sure what I was supposed to be doing, I had the drive to keep going and made me want to work harder.

The second is grit or what some might call determination. When you're home alone and no one is watching you, what are you doing to move the needle? What action are you taking every day to move your business forward? And like I said before, even when you put things out into the world, if they're not successful, keep going, keep moving forward and that grit, that determination or maybe just gumption has helped me stay in business this long.

The final skill that I think is essential, and one I think I already had, is treating your team and clients like you would want to be treated. Corny? Maybe, but I've had clients that have stayed with me since day one, because I've taken a vested interest in their businesses. I talk with them like they're humans, not just like a revenue stream. Next, build a team full of people that you would want to hang out with, people who you'd go have dinner and drinks with….people that you like, that your clients will like. Pay them well, and treat them with the dignity and respect they deserve and they'll stay with you a long time. I've had team members who have been around for 5+ years. That's practically unheard of for an online agency. It's because we have fun, have boundaries and treat each other with respect.

▶ **What was the greatest mindset or identity shift you had to have to be as successful as you are?**

Two shifts I still need to conquer: mindset and identity. To begin with, you're just one of many in the online world, so you do need to stand out, and to do that, you have to put yourself out into the world. That can be super scary, haters are going to come after you and you're going to have to get thick skin.

That means recognizing that you're not for everyone, so don't try to be (hello…know your audience). And get comfortable being uncomfortable. It's part of the gig. If you're going to do business online, people are going to have to see you and hear from you. But don't get discouraged when you see the nasty comments or people thinking you look or sound ridiculous. You're not for everyone and that is OK.

That phrase from Field of Dreams, "If you build it they will come,"….yeah, that doesn't happen online. You can't just build a website, put up some social media and hope to build an agency. You're going to have to get ready to be uncomfortable. Embrace the challenge and think of it like a task, just something that has to get done, but don't let that become your identity or let people change who you are because they don't like one post.

Finally, as an entrepreneur, mindset is key. Nobody comes to check on you, nobody comes to ask how you're doing, nobody asks how your day is going or what they can help you with. It can sometimes feel like you're on an island alone, going through all the highs and lows by yourself. Once I realized there is an entire world of other entrepreneurs out there going through the same things, I found a community where I felt like I could be myself and share stories. It didn't feel so lonely. Find your entrepreneurial people, they may be a mastermind, in a local networking group or in an online community. But find others who are on this journey - you'll be glad you did.

Being an agency owner isn't for the faint of heart, but it is by far the most rewarding and amazing experience that I've had in business. I hope that this combination of highly skilled agency owners has given you the motivation needed to see the real, the raw truth yet motivated you to step into your own personal agency owner greatness. Good Luck!

If you want to learn more about our agency and free resources we have available, visit our website at **https://digitaldawnagency.com**

My Gold Nugget Takeaways

Chapter 14
Mark Stern

Mark Stern is the founder of the Custom Box Agency and TeleportQR. Recently, he was featured in Forbes as one of the Next 1,000 Entrepreneurs redefining the American Dream.

Before becoming an entrepreneur, Mark was a top-ranked strategy consultant at Deloitte Consulting, the world's largest consulting firm.

Mark holds an MBA from Duke University. He is a five-time Spartan Trifecta holder, South-by-Southwest Start-up Mentor, and lifetime lover of tacos and BBQ. Mark currently lives in Austin, Texas.

I left Corporate America unexpectedly in 2018. I was weeks away from being promoted to Jr. Partner at a top five consulting firm, and everything changed in December 2017.

The Christmas holiday was the first time I was able to slow my brain down from a year's worth of nonstop fire drills. I thrive in chaos, but I didn't realize how disconnected I was to myself. I lost my own sense of identity. And then one night a woke up with tears in my eyes. I had premonition that if I continued down the pathway I was, on, it will kill me. I can honestly say that I've never experienced anything like this ever in my life, but I'll never forget what it felt like.

On January 3rd, 2018, I met my Partner in Dallas, Texas, and officially put in my notice. At the time, I had no backup plan, no side hustle or even an inkling that I'd ever be an agency owner. And I carried with me over $65,000 in student loan debt from business school.

What I did believe was that once I transitioned away from corporate america, I'd be able to rediscover who Mark Stern truly is. I'd be able to free up the mental capacity to make way for something greater. And this journey led me down the pathway that I'm on today. It has led me to create the Custom Box Agency and discover something that fulfills me every day.

This chapter is broken down into four parts that will guide you through the last few years of growing my agency. And hopefully a part of my story will also become a part of yours.

Part One: Who Are You?
Part Two: Are You Good At What You Do?
Part Three: Is Your Business Dependent On You?
Part Four: Are You Ready For What's Next?

At the end of each part, take some time to reflect on the challenge. This section is for YOU to not only read the content, but to apply it to your own business.

Know that I want you to TAKE ACTION.

We entrepreneurs choose to take on a heavy burden for those we serve, and the world needs us. What we do is hard, but we do it because we know we have a higher calling. For me, it's an innate desire to simplify the transformation of our clients and those they serve. But for you it may be something far greater that has yet to reveal itself. So are you ready to get started? Let's do this.

▶ PART ONE: WHO ARE YOU?

Everything in my business changed back in May 2020 when my mentor, Bart Miller, challenged me with three words:

WHO ARE YOU?

It was the single greatest piece of advice that made the biggest impact on my business. At the time, the COVID Pandemic launched the world into a new normal. Everyone was in lockdown due to quarantine, and the stress of uncertainty was imminent. I had two businesses that were starting to come to life...A coaching and done-for-you service for virtual events, and a new agency whose focus was building custom boxes.

I had just started to work with Bart when he made a simple observation. You see, Bart had reached out to some of my peers and asked them the question "Who is Mark?"

Half of the responses highlighted that I did virtual events. The other half indicated that I worked on custom boxes. To the market, I was perceived as 50% one thing and 50% another, and this was not good. When you try to be a little bit of everything, you'll quickly discover that you're a whole lotta nothing because you cannot clearly articulate your real value.

"Are you the virtual event guy or the custom box guy?" And that was it. I made the decision to go "All In" on Custom Boxes. That one decision truly changed my life.

When someone searches for recommendations, whether via word of mouth or social media, for people who do custom boxes, universally it made it *so much* easier for other people to recommend me. It also had another added benefit. I no longer needed to think about launching virtual events. I could dedicate all my mental capacity to how custom boxes can enhance the customer experience. I could test new concepts and develop a point of view that was so focused on my craft that it continued to help differentiate me in the marketplace.

Flash forward to a year later, and Custom Box Agency passed one million dollars in annual revenue. We were officially a multi seven-figure agency, and the best part is that we did not spend one dime on paid traffic. Our business has grown organically. It has grown from word of mouth.

So if you truly want to know WHO I AM, here's what I'd tell you:

I'm Mark Stern.
I live in Austin Texas, and I'm the Founder of Custom Box Agency.
We help our clients increase the lifetime value of their customers through direct mail – and our vehicle of choice is custom boxes and mailers.
We are innovative, and we're in the business of experience design.
We want our clients to be intentional about the customer journey, and we help them put the systems in place to simplify their customer's transformation.

So now it's your turn. Who are YOU?

▶ CHALLENGE #1: WHO ARE YOU?

Alright—so you probably know where I'm going with this.

You have 60 seconds to tell me what is it that you do. In fact, I want to know so badly that I'd like for you to send me a private VOICE MEMO on Facebook Messenger answering this one question…

WHO ARE YOU?

Facebook caps voice memos to 60 seconds, so it's the perfect opportunity to put it all on the line. As an agency owner, if you can clearly articulate your value proposition, you'll make it easier for people to understand who are you, what you do, and how you can help them.

▶ PART TWO: ARE YOU GOOD AT WHAT YOU DO?

Had you told me when I left Corporate America back in 2018 that I would pursue a lifelong dream of boxes, I would have said you've lost your mind. At the time, I was a process and strategy consultant at the world's largest consulting firm, Deloitte Consulting. And the truth was that I had no clue what I wanted to do with my life. But the reality was the writing was always on the wall.

In college, I was the president of my class for all four years. I couldn't care less about the title—what I wanted was the opportunity to create experiences that brought my fellow classmates together.

Following graduation, I moved to Chicago, Illinois, to work for an Experiential Marketing agency in the beverage space. We designed experiences around some of the leading brands to help our dream customers develop a stronger connection to us. We wanted to create memories and be buzzworthy. Even at Deloitte, I worked with clients in the retail, fitness, hotel, and gaming industries to build the strategy for the customer experience of the future. Whether I realized it or not at the time, the reality is that everything I've done had lead me to where I am today.

Custom Box Agency is not in the business of building swag boxes. In fact, we often joke with our clients that SWAG means "Stuff Without A Goal." Don't get me wrong. Swag definitely has its place, but we believe swag makes the most sense when you've established community and connection.

Instead, we challenge our clients to be intentional with how they're using the Direct Mail channel. Send your customers the tools and resources they need to accelerate their ability to achieve the "desired outcome" of your products and services. Again, give them what they need to simplify their transformation–the entire reason why they started working with you in the first place. And you know what? We're not just great at what we do. We're World-class.

The better we understand what our clients are trying to do, the more we're able to help them realize that outcome. Our goal is NOT to pivot or distract our clients from their core business goals. We aim to amplify what they're doing. If I were to identify the biggest contributing factor to our success, it would be that we unconditionally and unequivocally belief in our product. We are our biggest advocate. And when you "get" exactly what it is we do, it will change the way you think about your business.

The plight of the entrepreneur is a difficult one.

I'd be lying if I said that I never experienced highs and lows. The first few years of entrepreneurship are like sitting on a never-ending rollercoaster. But every time I had doubt or wanted to "throw in the towel," I'd ask myself two questions:

+ Are you good at what you do?
+ Does what you offer transform lives?

And sure enough, these two questions have a POWERFUL way to almost instantly change my state and remind me why I do what I do. Our custom box experiences have saved lives. They've also changed the way clients "show up" and serve their customers. Most importantly, the world needs what we have to offer. And we're just getting started.

▶ CHALLENGE #2: ARE YOU GOOD AT WHAT YOU DO?

So the question at hand, *"Are you good at what you do?" is* really an important one. The reality is if you do not believe that you are good at what you do… or what you have to offer… why should anyone else believe in you? Belief starts within you.

The second question: Does what you offer transform lives?

…is equally as important. And here's why.

If you are great at what you do, and if what you have to offer transforms lives, then I believe that you have an obligation to get loud and do whatever it takes to serve those who need you most.

You may be the key to save someone else's life.

So get out of your head and share your gifts with the world. Whenever you are in a self-sabotage or limited mindset, I want you to do the following exercise (and this is the same exercise that I take myself and my clients through).

Pick up a blank piece of paper and pen and WRITE DOWN:
I am GREAT at what I do.
What I offer TRANSFORMS LIVES.

Read it out loud. Hear yourself say these words. And if you truly believe these words, you will find power within them. Don't overthink this exercise. Just do it. And after you do it, I challenge you to snap a picture with this message, post it on social media, and tag me on it.

▶ PART THREE: IS YOUR BUSINESS DEPENDENT ON YOU?

In March 2022, I spent a week with Russell Brunson's Inner Circle Mastermind in Riviera Maya. If you were to ask me what my single biggest take away, it was a 2-minute conversation with my good friend Justin Wubben.

At the time, Justin and I had barely spoken to one another, but after a small mastermind hosted by our very own Stephanie Dove Blake, Justin pulled me aside and asked me the question…

Do you have a good business?

I responded, "I believe I have a GREAT business. I love what I do."

Then he asked me…

Could your business survive without you?

I sat there and processed the question. Could Custom Box Agency continue to survive without me, or is the business truly dependent on me? I shrugged, to which he responded, "Then you don't have a great business."

Woof.

These words struck me right in the gut, and I couldn't stop thinking about them for weeks following the interaction. The heart of these questions is important for any business or agency owner.

If I were to disappear tomorrow, do I have the people and systems in place to allow my business to thrive? The truth is the success of Custom Box Agency cannot be dependent on one person. It's simply not fair to my team, my clients, and those that they serve.

And this leads to one of the most important skills you need to develop to be a successful business owner.

The art of letting go of full control and empowering others.

When you start to grow your business, it will start to sprout its own arms and legs that will become so much larger than you. Custom Box Agency may have started with a team of two (thank you Becky for being a part of this crazy adventure), but it has since evolved to become a movement brought to life by an amazing team and clients we get to work with every day. It would be selfish of me to stunt its potential growth and impact by getting in my own way.

And I'll share with you one of the BEST DECISIONS I've ever made to help empower my team.

It started in October 2021 when I flew my entire leadership team down to Austin for a little retreat. Up to that point, all of our interactions had been limited to zoom only. But when I flew the team down to Austin, something magical happened. And it's changed the course of our business.

The leadership team came together to completely redesign our client experience and deliver process. And I barely said a word throughout the retreat. The team took control of the future of the business, and they looked to me for guidance, direction, and approval.

It made me realize that I need to get out of my own way. The Custom Box Agency has a strong mission, vision, and culture. But what makes us so incredible is the team of individuals who make dreams come true.

Since October 2021, Custom Box Agency flies team members into Texas at least once a quarter. Each time we're together, we tackle a new business objective, and every time the outcome of these sessions change the trajectory of our business.

It's so powerful that I cannot stress the importance of bringing your team in at least once throughout the year. You may think that it's too expensive to bring the team together, as flights, hotel, and food can really start to add up. But the truth is that every time we do this, whatever it costs to host the retreat, it comes back to our business ten-fold as it is a catalyst for business development and innovation. And the more you empower your team, the faster you can build an enterprise that is not dependent on you to thrive.

▶ CHALLENGE #3: IS YOUR BUSINESS DEPENDENT ON YOU?

Let's talk about getting you out of your business. Speak with any successful agency owner and they'll tell you to start to build your team well before you think you're ready to. It's okay to start small and grow gradually, but spend the time to hire individuals who can quickly take time-consuming tasks off your plate. This frees you up to truly work on your business (and things that move the needle forward) and not in your business.

So what is Challenge #3? If you were to host a team retreat next week, what would be the #1 objective you'd want to accomplish? Build the agenda and identify members of your team who can lead the different sessions. Who should be there? Why?

For the Custom Box Agency, past retreats have focused on topics such as:

- Optimizing our 12-week Custom Box Delivery Process
- Redesigning our Client Experience (from Discovery to In Market)
- Identifying New Business Capabilities to bring to market
- Introducing New Systems to Scale our Business Model

Keep this exercise simple, and when you're ready, make it happen. Choose a location and a date and go. It changed my business, and I'm confident it'll do the same for you, too.

▶ PART FOUR: ARE YOU READY FOR WHAT'S NEXT?

Momentum is an incredible thing.

When I think back to the past two years, it's a surreal and humbling experience to reflect on the journey I've been on. We grew the Custom Box Agency to a multi seven-figure business in less than two years, and we did it via word of mouth only. At the time this chapter was written, we have not spent a dime on paid traffic. We also have no investors.

And in that time, we've…

- Produced well over 100 Custom Box and Mailer experiences.
- Built a team of 20+ employees throughout the US and Globe
- Launched a warehouse and fulfillment center in Austin, Texas
- Launched two software platforms: TeleportQR and CBA Dash (Inventory Management Platform)
- Shipped 10,000s of boxes and mailers all across the globe

We've also been recognized by Forbes as one of the Next 1,000 Entrepreneurs Redefining the American Dream and received two (2) ClickFunnels Two Comma Club Awards. We've even been featured in best-selling books and publications for our work. And we're just getting started.

I highlight these achievements for one reason only. Your life can change overnight. Two years ago, I didn't have a business. I didn't have any two comma club awards. I was an aspiring entrepreneur who was trying to figure it out. And in many ways, I still believe I'm an aspiring entrepreneur.

▶ **What was the greatest mindset or identity shift you had to have to be as successful as you are?**

The greatest mindset shift I had was realized by others before I was able to see it myself. So here's the secret...

**The world around you wants you to succeed. We want you to win.
People need what you have to offer.
Your worst enemy is the small voice between your ears.
It's you, and you need to get out of your own way.**

And until you realize that, you simply won't be ready for what's next. I needed a mentor to call me out when I got in a self-sabotaging head space. I needed masterminds and communities of like entrepreneurs to help guide me through the unknown. But for me, experience is at the heart of what simplifies transformation. And I'm honored to be surrounded everyday by a team and clients who inspire me all the time.

So get out of your own way, and get ready to embrace what's next.

▶ **CHALLENGE #4: ARE YOU READY FOR WHAT'S NEXT?**

So are you ready for what's next? Mindset is easily 80% of the game for agency owners and entrepreneurs. You HAVE to be in the right headspace to launch and grow your movement. If you do not have a mentor, go find one.

In my own experience, mentorship is one of the most powerful ways to reset your mindset and keep you accountable and focused on your core business objectives.

Here are a few items to consider when selecting a mentor:

- Can you articulate WHY you want this individual as a mentor? What do they offer? What is the structure of their program?

- Have they achieved success in areas similar to what you're currently doing?

- What level of access do you have to them (i.e., weekly one-on-ones)? Will they be able to really get into your business? Or are they hands off (i.e., group coaching)?

- Do they have a community? If so, will there be any activities designed to bring the community together in person?

- Are they actively asking you to set goals? If so, do they hold you accountable?

- Have you connected with other individuals who have been mentored by this guide?

- Do you trust them?

Mark Stern is the founder of the Custom Box Agency. Visit **www.customboxagency.com** to launch your custom box or custom mailer today.

My Gold Nugget Takeaways

Chapter 15
Preston Schmidli & McBilly Sy

Preston Schmidli started off in sales and marketing as the owner of an insurance brokerage. After falling on hard times, Preston resorted to selling his own blood to pay for gas, groceries, and marketing courses. Today, he is an award-winning entrepreneur and published author of the Amazon best seller, *If I Were You*. With his expertise in sales psychology and marketing strategy, Preston currently consults with mortgage professionals, helping them transform their lives and their communities for the better.

McBilly Sy is a first-generation immigrant who moved to the United States in search for a better future to help provide for his family. He climbed his way up the corporate ladder but eventually quit to start his own marketing agency after getting burned out working two full-time jobs. McBilly is now a business consultant, marketing coach, and an award-winning entrepreneur. He currently helps loan originators leverage online marketing and social media to scale their businesses and create long lasting, generational wealth for their clients and their families. Together, they run Good Vibe Squad Marketing, a multi-million-dollar agency exclusively serving Mortgage Professionals.

Hey, it's Preston Schmidli and McBilly Sy of Good Vibe Squad Marketing and we're a Growth Partner for Mortgage Professionals. We have an awesome marketing agency with an amazing team, all of whom are obsessed with creating the best experience for our clients that we can.

Our agency is very healthy now, but it wasn't always that way. We want to share some lessons with you about using "back-against-the-wall" moments as launchpads to do something wonderful with your life. You are capable of greatness, and we hope to inspire you with our stories. Let's go back to our start and tie the lessons in along the way.

McBilly and I (Preston) started into the marketing world from very different places. In his earlier years, McBilly was quite successful as a TV Show host and male model in the Philippines, but he felt that something was missing. Growing up with a single mom and a few siblings, he felt a deep desire to reconnect with his father who had moved to California when he was 9. At the age of 20, he found himself with the opportunity to visit California and meet his father again, this time, as a man.

McBilly was only planning to visit the United States for a few months and then return to a show they were producing, but once in America, McBilly realized that even though his life was already pretty good in the Philippines, the opportunity in the United States was greater. He felt called to be in the US. He applied for his green card and began the pursuit of becoming an American citizen.

It was a radical shift, leaving his previous life behind. Once a television show host, he was now humbled by the reality of pushing carts at Lowe's Home Improvement while he figured out his life's direction. Doing what he needed to do to get by, he worked there until his Computer Science degree helped him land a job at a pathology lab during the day while also studying to get his Medical Technician license at night. This was the beginning of burning the candle at both ends to have a better life.

Eventually, McBilly completed his schooling and received his Medical Technician license, and with his newfound time he obtained a second job at a Hospital Blood Bank. He would start his day at the Pathology Lab working from 3PM to 11:30PM, and then he would go to the Hospital and work from midnight to 8AM. These 16-hour workdays wore on McBilly, and one foggy night in New York he had to confront the consequences of his lifestyle. While driving from one job to the next, deprived of sleep, McBilly hit black ice as he saw the brake lights flash on the car in front of him. He tried to brake, but the car kept moving.

Filled with adrenaline, he quickly turned the wheel to the side to avoid the car in front of him. Luckily, the tires managed to catch enough traction to avoid an accident. He pulled over, and in a sense, he saw his life flash before his own eyes. He asked himself the hard question, "McBilly, what are we doing with our life? Why are we doing this? This isn't the life I want."

Determined to use his technical skills elsewhere, McBilly knew it was time to bet on himself and go all in as an entrepreneur. A week later, he quit his first job. Two weeks after that, he quit his second job and jumped in with both feet trying to become a master marketer.

▶ **Quick Win: Focus on your zone of genius; that is where you are most needed in your business.**

Focus on your zone of genius, but also have exposure/familiarity with the rest of your business when you are starting out. Once you gain momentum, hire people and delegate the other components of your business so you can live in your zone of genius.

On the other side of the country, I (Preston) was facing a struggle of my own. I was already an entrepreneur, but I was selling my franchise insurance agency and creating my own independent brokerage from the ground up. Normally, the transition shouldn't be so bad, but what was supposed to be a three-month non-compete transition period was dragged out to nine months due to "legal technicalities." I wasn't interested in pursuing a legal battle I couldn't afford, so I spent the time learning marketing and working on building the brand of my soon-to-be independent brokerage because that was how I was planning to make money.

After three months, we were out of money. I was prepared to afford the 90 days, but I was not prepared to feed my family for the nine months it became. So, after exhausting all options we saw in front of us, my girlfriend Lacey and I started selling 2 liters of plasma every week to get gas money to go to the food bank, so we could put food on the table. McBilly and I joke that during this phase, we were both on "other ends of the needles." It was humbling to go through; I remember feeling so grateful that so many kind people put time into the food banks to provide for people who were in tough spots. I just didn't see myself as someone that would have needed the help of a food bank.

We did this for the greater part of a year until one day we came home from the food bank and the plasma center to a blue door hanger on the door. It was a notice from the power company that we had 48 hours to pay them $680 or else they were going to cut the power. I couldn't sell insurance like I was trained and ready to do, and I legally and physically couldn't sell enough plasma to pay this off... We had to throw a Hail Mary.

I had been using some of the plasma center money every month to pay for a marketing course I was taking to learn how to do my own lead generation and build marketing and automation systems. I loved doing it, but I had only learned how to do it for myself. The thought had never crossed my mind to offer marketing and lead generation services to anyone else.

But we didn't have a choice, the clock was ticking.

So, we scraped a list of 4,800 real estate agents using D7 Lead Finder, built a landing page offering lead generation services for $750/month. (We now charge $1,600+ per month, but we all start somewhere), and then we launched a cold email campaign from Mailshake.

▶ **Quick Win: Focus on strategy, not on tactics.**

The marketing world is full of tactics and shiny objects that will lead you astray. But if you focus on learning the strategy behind why the tactic worked, then you can apply that same strategy to your business or specific niche.

At this time for us it was cold emails, so you can imagine the negative responses that started coming in, but I was focused on working the engagement because I didn't have a choice. One man ended up hopping on a call with me, and he hired me. I processed his payment over the phone and the money hit our account two hours before the power company was going to cut the power. It was enough to pay the power company off, fill the gas tank and buy some food.

Most importantly, something in my brain flipped. I knew that marketing was going to be the future of my professional life. I started getting every book I could afford, and I became a very committed student.

Not long after both McBilly and I began to step into marketing, McBilly made a post in the Clickfunnels group asking a question about something specific to Real Estate Agents. Truthfully, I don't engage with a lot of posts in groups like that, but I guess it was the universe setting up a good thing. I saw his post and told him that I personally preferred working with Mortgage Professionals more and we started to shoot advice back and forth helping each other build funnels and grow our agencies.

▶ Quick Win: Invest in Mentors and Courses

Throughout our journey, we invested in mentors and courses and used them to get up to speed faster and to learn from others' mistakes. We used that mentorship as base knowledge and built upon it.

The time came for a mastermind in Puerto Rico that I was attending after scraping together a few thousand dollars to cover the cost. I had to; it was with a group of marketers who I loved studying with. I brought it up to McBilly and he really wanted to go, but he was in a similar situation–in debt because he was scammed by a marketer he was trying to learn from. He reached out to the host of the mastermind to ask if he could attend if he was able to get a few people to join his course, and he also offered to cover the mastermind for photos and video. The host agreed and McBilly was on his way to join the event too.

After a long weekend with McBilly and other marketers, he and I developed a deep connection. McBilly and I worked well together, but it took us coming out of our element to work together to realize that we might be onto something big here. He had a great demo slide deck, I was used to doing a one-call close on the phone, and we agreed that if we teamed up using his deck and my one-call close, we could probably do well. As a failsafe I told him that we could use my traffic since I had a bunch of leads.

We booked 2 calls back-to-back with Loan Officers and with our combined efforts closed them both to earn our first $3,000 working together. From that point, we locked arms in business and never looked back.

Here's the thing: we made a commitment early on to create the most valuable service that we could provide for our clients (Mortgage Professionals). We have always had a strong belief that we're the best at what we do because we give so much to our clients within our service. This gives us the conviction that we need to stand tall in our offer.

▶ Quick Win: Understand Your Clients

Interview your clients religiously and put yourself in your clients' shoes so you can truly understand their pain points and how you can help solve their problems. There is no shortcut here. This is the benefit of "niching" down to a core audience that you serve so you can truly solve their problems. This is the reason why we niched down to only serving mortgage loan officers.

Years have gone by, and we have done many cool things together, but we've worked together to grow past the multi-million dollar level and now we have our targets set on $10,000,000 per year.

That took half of a decade for us to get to. More importantly, it took both of us having our backs against the wall and being forced to action. It was as if we were being called to war in our own lives, to reclaim our dreams. It's easy in those moments to feel like life is against you. But sometimes it's the much-needed catalyst for big and powerful change.

▶ Quick Win: The customer is not always right.

When you're starting out, it's easy to be a "yes man" or "yes woman" since you don't have the authority you might feel you need to stand your ground. However, it's important to remember that your clients are hiring you because you either know something that they don't, or because you are better than they are at marketing. We saw more clients having success with our program when we started to set boundaries within our service and hold them accountable to their actions. This can sometimes mean having an uncomfortable conversation with clients, but as long as you are transparent, they will appreciate it more often than not.

With that said, our advice is to go "all-in" when you are at a challenging place in your life. Be incredibly bold. It doesn't require a "rock bottom" moment or a mid-life crisis, although those are great places to bet on yourself in a big way.

The beauty of having your back against a wall is that there is nowhere left to run. You can't maintain your old patterns. It confronts your identity and forces you to adapt or die. I would not have become a marketer if I wasn't FORCED to stop selling insurance. McBilly probably wouldn't have become a marketer if it wasn't for the moment that working two jobs, starved of sleep, almost killed him. We knew in our hearts that we had to show up and fight for ourselves and that we had to do things that were very uncomfortable and new. Having your back against the wall makes you next-level resourceful, which is a common and required trait amongst every masterful and successful marketer that we know.

Being a great marketer is a lot of work—mostly mental. All our good friends who are very successful came from nothing or close to it. They earned every dollar they have with hard work, and they kept working hard even when they didn't see the money right away.

▶ **In Summary, here are the takeaways:**
6. Be bold. Lean into the moments in life where your back is against the wall.

7. Be resourceful. Everything you need is within and around you already.

8. Be patient and keep working hard. Success takes years, and there are far too many people that try to sell you "overnight success" with courses or ideas. Everything you need to be successful is already within you, waiting to be unlocked.

9. Be humble when you start having success. It's best to actively work on gratitude for the things you have.

10. Be committed to the long game. Don't take your foot off the gas, keep doing what makes you successful until you can hire, and train and delegate it to someone else (that hopefully does it better than you) so that you can focus on the next thing.

▶ **BONUS: Delegate as much as you can.**

If you find yourself saying things like "It's just easier if I do it myself," or "No one will do it as good as I will," then *you* are the bottleneck in your business, and your growth will be limited until you overcome these thoughts.

If you would like to learn more about us, go to **www.goodvibesquad.com**.

On that page are videos that detail how we help Mortgage Professionals grow their businesses. If you look a little further you will also find our free book called the *Billion Dollar Mortgage Playbook* to download. It has tips and tricks that we learned from the journey to help our more than 500 clients fund over $2 billion dollars' worth of loans at the time of this writing.

Good luck, and if you would like to connect, reach out to us on Facebook and/or Instagram.

My Gold Nugget Takeaways

Chapter 16
Stephanie Dove Blake

Stephanie Dove Blake is a 2 Comma Club award winning, recognized marketer, speaker, author, and coach with a docket of praise from industry-shifting marketing experts like Russell Brunson, Billy Gene, and Julie Chenell. But more important to her, she's helped hundreds of her clients build their businesses and make the impact they're destined for.

Stephanie started her agency in 2016 as a struggling homeschooling momma of 4. Against all odds, this high school dropout, techie-geek grew a 7-figure agency from scratch and has made waves in the industry.

Accolades and accomplishments are one thing; what makes Stephanie a true unicorn is her love for people paired with a fierce dedication to building a business while keeping her family first.

Stephanie brings passion, strategy, inspiration and brilliant creativity to whatever she puts her hands to. Stephanie is the wife to a red-bearded hero, mother to 4 out-of-the-box blessings and a lover of all things Jesus, marketing, *Back to the Future*, *Princess Bride* and Blue Bell® Ice Cream.

▶ **What was the greatest piece of advice you received from a mentor or coach that made the biggest impact in your agency journey?**

This is a really tough question for me to answer. I've had so many incredible mentors and coaches that have given me game-changing wisdom: Russell Brunson, Billy Gene, Teresa Kwon, Julie Chenell, Katie Richardson, Nik Robbins, Robb Bailey, Shawn Dill and Lacey Book and more.

When I think about the one that has stuck with me the most, that has had the BIGGEST impact on my agency journey and my life, that title goes to a man who's not currently in the digital marketing space: Brian Allen. He's someone you've likely never heard of unless you live in Oklahoma.

One day at a dinner almost a decade ago, way before I had started my agency, he said, "You know, Stephanie, starting a business is a lot like going to a pet store and picking out a really cute baby alligator. It's adorable at first and it starts growing and you teach it a few tricks, and then one day, you wake up and you realize that your cute baby alligator is now as BIG AS YOU! And... it's gnawing on your leg and threatening to swallow you WHOLE!"

That story stuck with me. Brian had started multiple businesses and had been a part of numerous companies and I trusted him. When I started my agency, I pictured my new baby alligator and I was determined to grow it into the tamest alligator I could.

When I pictured my life as an entrepreneur where the business was consuming me, I pictured loss of connection with my husband and children due to limited time and stress. I pictured a deep kind of loneliness where I was working and toiling for success in the sight of others and my own standards yet being a **devastating failure at home**.

What is a million-dollar business worth just to lose what you love most?

You can't buy back time that you've lost with those that matter to you, so as I built and continue to build today, that thought is in the forefront of my mind. I have certainly not gone as fast as I could have, and that was by choice.

★ I choose to be a present mother.
★ I choose to pour into the relationship with my handsome red-bearded hero of a husband.
★ I choose to say no to external pressure to sacrifice unredeemable time with the ones I love.

Contrary to a lot of advice out there, your children WILL suffer the consequences of your absence or lack of intentional presence. There's a lot of people who say, "they'll understand when they're older. It's ok to sacrifice because you're giving them what you never had." I call BS.

Family is important and your presence matters. Your fully-there presence matters. I'm just going to say it again in case you read right past it:

✦Your presence MATTERS✦

My encouragement to you is that, whether you are picking out your baby alligator or you've already lost a limb, it's never too early or too late to set boundaries and regain control. The ones you love are worth the fight for both an excellent business and an excellent home life.

▶ **What would you say was the biggest contributing factor to your success?**

You never know how ONE new relationship in your life could drastically change the entire trajectory of your life. That one relationship for me was meeting a fierce woman named Madlin Mangrum at a homeschooling conference when I was an exasperated, lonely, scared, newly homeschooling mom who was running on fumes and looking for hope. What I learned from Madlin was, what I believe is the BIGGEST contributing factor to my success.

When I met Madlin, she was a Strengths Finder coach. While Madlin has a gift of understanding people that oozes from her pores, she had also studied the strengths and weaknesses we as humans have: 34 to be exact, according to Gallup's Strengths Finder Assessment.

As a member of her team years before I started my agency, she paid for my test to learn what my top strengths were. When I first saw them, I didn't really understand the significance, but as I dove in with Madlin and learned more, it was like seeing myself for the first time.

My top strengths are:

- ◆ Includer
- ◆ Positivity
- ◆ Achiever
- ◆ Input
- ◆ Communication

Madlin taught me that the world tells us to find our weaknesses and focus on them so we can improve. Instead, Madlin taught me two lessons which I will reveal, but I must tell you a short story first. (This story is paraphrased from Gallup Strengthsfinder, www.gallup.com)

Here's how the story goes. There were two groups of readers in a high school: "Gifted" and "Normal." The Gifted group was reading at a remarkably high rate, 350 words per minute. The second group–the Normal group–were reading at 90 words per minute. In this study, both groups were given the same speed-reading course.

Here is what happened:
After the "Normal" group–who was originally reading at 90 words per minute–went through the speed-reading course, they improved to about 150 words per minute, or about a 66% increase.

That's pretty incredible! However, even more incredible is what happened with the "Gifted" group of kids. Remember the kids reading at 350 words per minute? Do you think it went down, stayed the same, or went up?

Here is what happened:
The gifted group's reading speed improved to 2,900 words per minute from the original 350wpm. That's an 828% increase!! They saw an 828% improvement by taking a speed-reading course when they were already gifted in reading! Now, what can we learn from this?

▶ **Lesson #1: There is more room to improve in your areas of natural talent than in your areas of weakness.**

When the gifted readers focused on improving their area of strength, they grew exponentially more, which is absolutely contrary to our natural tendency to focus on improving weaknesses.

As I began to understand the power of each of my strengths and focused on them, I experienced true transformation. It was slow transformation, but a TRUE, forever kind of change. I realized that I LIVE for helping people feel seen and heard at the core of who I am (Includer). I want to help people believe in themselves and find the call on their lives. As one who has the strength of "Positivity," I can find my way out of dark, hard situations and I can help lead others to do the same. There is NO WALL.

Because I'm an "Achiever," I know that I'm going to show up and MAKE. IT. HAPPEN. It's what I do. It's in my bones. Having "Input" as a top strength enables me to consume information and collect the things that I learn but then my strength of "Communication" drives me to want to share it with others… and do so in a way that makes an impact.

Knowing these strengths has helped me understand where to focus my energies so that I can find FULFILLMENT in the midst of my work and really see my strengths shine. Lesson #2 was the real kicker though.

▶ Lesson #2: Identify Your Kryptonite.

With the Strengths Finder assessment finding out your top 5 strengths is only $19.99 but you can pay more to "unlock" the list of your 34 strengths. I had only focused on my top five strengths but when I unlocked all 34 strengths and saw what was at the BOTTOM of the list (my weaknesses), I had revelation after revelation.

Specifically, one "strength" at the bottom of my list really opened my eyes: Consistency. It's #33 on my list. That's almost dead last! I had felt the effects of consistency being a weakness of mine before, but I hadn't actually realized the depth at which I was subconsciously sabotaging things because of my avoidance of doing things consistently.

I could have chosen to start to work on my consistency strength and get better at it, but this isn't what Gallup's Strengths Finder test is for.

I had just learned what my kryptonite was. Before, it was getting the better of me. Now, I *knew* better so I could then *do* better by hiring people around me to pick up the tasks that needed consistency.

This was a game changer! I also learned that the strength of "Deliberation" was at the bottom of my list as well. The "Deliberation" strength is when someone takes serious care in making decisions or choices. They're careful and vigilant. I, on the other hand, am risk tolerant. I do not deliberate long on decisions. I MOVE.

Because of this, it could be a blind spot for me. So I have hired people to work with me on decision making that DO deliberate. They think through all the things and help me slow down a bit (if I listen) before taking action.

On our team I've had all team members take the Strengths Finder test. Over the years we have also gone on to include Myers Briggs Testing (16 Personalities), DISC Assessments, Enneagram, Love Languages, and more. It has been powerful for Social Sparrow but also hugely impactful on the growth of each one of our team members.

When you're building your agency, those you surround yourself with as your team is everything. You can't scale without a solid foundation.

Knowing yourself thoroughly isn't just a business strategy... it's something that I believe <u>you owe to yourself</u>.

Find out what gifts you've been given and unleash them into the world while being wise in knowing your weaknesses. It helps you LOVE others well, break through the things that hold you back and realize the call on your life.

▶ **What is the greatest skill you needed to develop to be as successful as you are?**

As an agency owner we must be out-of-the-box thinkers, problem solvers, and fire-putter-outers. Most agency owners I've met are like me. We actually THRIVE on last minute deadlines, emergency situations and finding creative solutions to problems. It's not that we seek them out (well... some of us do), but when there is a problem, we CAN and WILL solve it. It's what we do. It's in our DNA.

This is a gift, BUT it's also a bit of a curse. As I was getting my legs underneath me as an agency owner, my day could include ANYTHING. I might be building a landing page, creating an ad campaign, doing a sales call, talking to a frustrated client, or creating a training. Additionally, in my circumstance at that time, it could also mean teaching math to a frustrated 4th grader, starting a load of laundry, making lunch, and doing the dishes. The bottom line was this: whatever needed my attention got it. If there was a problem, I had the answer.

I saw NO WALL. Fire after fire, I put them out. I didn't know it at the time, but I was developing a healthy addiction to the dopamine hits that come when you function day-to-day like that.

That is what built my agency. However, it's also what almost destroyed my agency as well. At an event, Alex Charfen talked to us about doing a Time Study to discover what was causing pressure and noise in our lives. He said something so profound: "What got you to where you are today might kill you going forward."

And that was exactly what was happening. My ability to pivot, problem solve and put out fires was what enabled me to multi-task and make my agency a reality, but it was going to keep me STUCK in the same position if I didn't adapt, learn and grow.

At the time I was experiencing a TON of pressure and noise and I needed to determine what was happening. I would wake up, start my day with my to-do list and before I knew it, the day was over, and my to-do list was untouched. I felt like a million bucks because I felt like I had slayed the day but ultimately, I was failing. I couldn't move balls forward anymore. The agency wasn't growing, and I knew it.

So I did a time study like Alex Charfen suggested. It was one of the HARDEST THINGS EVER. I absolutely HATED doing it. For 2 weeks, every 15 minutes I wrote down exactly what I was doing. Did I mention how much I really detest consistency?!? Ugh! But I did it... and within the first few days something was VERY, VERY, crystal clear.

I was chasing dopamine hits. I was consistently choosing to do ANYTHING other than the things on my to-do list. Those things were typically longer projects that took more DEEP work and creative energy. The gratification I'd get from those actions were delayed whereas when I would pop in and solve a client problem, I got a quick dopamine hit because I "saved the day."

I was addicted. My undiagnosed ADD was having a hay day. Just like an addict, I would KNOW that I needed to do the things on my list... I KNEW how important they were, but instead, I'd go check SLACK®, messenger, Voxer®, and Facebook®... subconsciously searching for my next hit/reason to not have to focus on the deep work.

I'd love to tell you that I've 100% conquered this skill BUT it's actually a different skill that I've developed that's made the BIGGEST difference in being able to KILL the dopamine hit addiction.

AWARENESS

Instead of flying by the seat of my pants in my perceived zone of problem-solving genius, I have learned to be AWARE of what I'm doing and why I'm doing it.

Snapping out of autopilot and into INTENTIONAL action is a SKILL and it starts with being able to be aware that you're doing it so that you can take action to KILL the addiction to the dopamine hits.

→ This looks like evaluating my day beforehand.

→ Being hyper focused on the top 3 things I need to do that day.

→ Turning off all distractions.

At one time I had an hourly check in set on my phone to make sure I was where I intended to be. Even now as I'm writing this, I have noise canceling headphones on (because my brain focuses on every noise and voice in my house), I have one Google Doc browser window open in FULL screen, *Do Not Disturb* is on, my phone is in my bedroom, and my family knows that momma is doing deep work.

I've stopped myself at least 8 times from going to check things or look things up that my brain went off on a tangent on. It's still a struggle, but I have awareness that one of my greatest strengths can also become one of my greatest weaknesses in continuing to build my business.

I hope that if any part of this resonated with you, that you, too, find out how to hack yourself and raise your awareness to what is holding you back from focusing on what really moves the needle forward in your business.

▶ **What was the greatest mindset or identity shift you had to have to be as successful as you are?**

The entrepreneurial journey is something you can't really know until you are living it. Here is a concept that surfaces often in Russell's Inner Circle:

There is no finish line for the majority of us.

The horizon (goal line) is always moving. We're creators and problem solvers by nature. As long as there is a problem to solve, we're not done.

As long as there is an idea in our head, creation will continue.

We tend to get into the mindset that if X happens (insert major goal here), then Z will follow (insert major reward or life altering status). Then we finally reach X as planned, and Z wasn't what we thought it was at all. Then we reset after deciding that we actually need to hit Y and THEN Z would finally happen. This is the wrong way of thinking for the entrepreneur.

A paradigm shift is needed, or we miss the fact that the JOURNEY is what it is all about, not the destination.

Business building is a numbers and goal-achieving endeavor. We can very easily lose sight of this and keep thinking that the next goal is the destination, when in reality, living the journey is the goal.

The Bible says in Proverbs 13:12, "hope deferred makes the heart sick" (NKJV). When we are constantly reaching for a goal, we attain it and consequently uncover a whole new set of problems to solve at that point which ultimately gives us a brand new goal. If we don't stop and celebrate reaching our original, now faded goal, it can feel like you're on a hamster wheel. Like Proverbs says, it really can make our heart sick when our hope is set on reaching a finish line that doesn't actually exist. However, if we grasp the concept that reaching a goal isn't the answer, it's the *doing along the way*, it changes everything.

When I started my agency, my goal was simply to provide some income for our family while working from home. Next my ability to dream grew! I dreamed that maybe I could "bring my husband home" and we did. Maybe I could reach 20 clients… and we did. Maybe I could grow an incredible team… and we did. Maybe I could build a 7-figure agency… and we did. Maybe I could start coaching… and I did.

You see, as we go along in the entrepreneurial journey, our capacity to hold bigger and bigger dreams grows. The present time YOU can't comprehend what the journey will have for you even in 5 years.

That's why we have to lean in and trust the journey.

This mindset shift for me has brought peace in the midst of raging storms because I know in my "knower" that I have been made <u>resilient</u>. If my agency blew up and I had nothing left, with God's help, I would find a way. When you know this about yourself, in a way you become bullet proof because you can trust that no matter what comes, you will overcome, adapt, and grow.

The key is to take our eyes off of a *goal* as a *destination*. The *destination* is right where you are. Here. Now.

Trust yourself to move forward into your calling every day, knowing that no matter what happens, no matter what POO hits the fan, no matter what people do, or if you fail, YOU. WILL. FIGURE. IT. OUT.

Why? Because you are resilient. You were born for this. You don't have to freak out when things don't go as planned. Everything will work for you as long as you get up and KEEP going.

You know you will. You will get up and keep going because that's what you have done up until now. Whether it's a failure or success, it leads you to the next step in the journey.

Rooting for You!

Stephanie Dove Blake

www.stephaniedoveblake.com

My Gold Nugget Takeaways

The Owners

Chapter 17
What's Next?

"Formal education will make you a living;
self-education will make you a fortune."
- Jim Rohn

Congratulations on making it this far in the book! By doing so, you have proven that you are serious about growing your marketing agency and building a life of true financial freedom.

You've learned a lot but now what?

Likely you've picked up this book and have read this far because you want *(or need)* something to change in your business. The truth is, real change never happens simply because you consume more knowledge. Transformation always follows action.

The Agency Titans that have contributed to this book have spent years struggling and overcoming the same exact obstacles you are going through today in your own marketing agency.

When it comes to running a digital marketing agency, there are no unique problems. Every problem you can find in your business is common to every marketing agency in the world. And as you've seen by going through this book, the answers you need are out there. It's just a matter of knowing which questions to ask and where you can find the right guidance to help you navigate the uncharted waters you find yourself in today.

If your intention is to build a marketing agency that you are no longer a slave to, one that serves you and your family and not the other way around...

If you dream of one day having a world-class team of generals that can think for themselves, innovate and drive outcomes for your business without your input.

If you hope that someday soon you will be able to truly take a vacation where you can honestly, truthfully step away from your business and know deep in your heart that your clients are being taken care of at the highest level so you can simply relax with your family...

If you never again want to experience the crippling feeling of financial anxiety that comes with not knowing which of your clients are going to default this month...

If you want to make the greatest impact you possibly can in the lives and businesses of your dream clients and are willing to do whatever it takes to see them win...

If that's you, then Stephanie and I (Franco) want to help.

Stephanie and I have both been through the gauntlet of building a successful marketing agency that affords a lifestyle of true financial freedom. Together, we have helped hundreds of entrepreneurs build successful businesses, many of which have grown to 6 and 7-figures using some of the very same strategies you've learned within the pages of this book.

The reason that we have compiled this book for you is to give you practical strategies that will help you on your journey to 7-figures with your marketing agency. And while that's helpful, it's not everything you need if you want to build a successful business.

Success is a formula made up of 3 key pillars:

1. Strategy

The first key pillar is Strategy. There is a saying that goes, *"You will never catch the sunset if you're running East."* What this means is that it doesn't matter how hard you are working or how many hours you put into something if what you're doing isn't working. You could be working 16 hour days and half-days on the weekends and still never make it past $20,000 per month. Is it due to lack of effort? Absolutely not, no one works harder than you. It's because you're working on things that add no value to your business and do not bring you closer to your ultimate goal of building a Limitless Agency.

This book is filled to the brim with effective strategies to grow your marketing agency. These strategies are proven and have worked for the Agency Titans and have helped them build their fortunes. But which one will work for you?

2. Skills

The second key pillar is Skills. We have, as a society, been grossly misled by the education system to believe that the world cares even an ounce about the effort that we put into our work. You think the world cares that you've worked 16 hours today? Do you think the marketplace is going to somehow compensate you for the fact that you pulled an all-nighter to hit a client deadline? No, the world rewards results. That's how the world works. If you provide value to the marketplace, the marketplace will reward you for that. It does not matter how many hours you devote to a project or goal, it only matters if you achieved it.

It's not enough to just know what the right thing to do is and then to do it. You have to do it well. You have to build up the skills that you need to be able to pull off the strategy effectively. You could have the greatest playwright in the world create the most wonderful play to be performed on the grandest stage with the warmest of all audiences, and if you have a terrible lead actor, it's all in vain. The second key pillar to being successful when it comes to growing your marketing agency to 7-figures is to develop the skills that you need to execute the strategy you've chosen effectively.

3. Self-confidence

The last key pillar is the most important. It is self-confidence. If you know what the right thing to do is (Strategy) and you are talented enough to effectively execute on it (Skills) but lack the self-confidence to get started… all hope is lost.

Stephanie and I created this book, not just to share the best Strategies that are working for marketing agencies today and not just to help you uplevel the skills that you'll need to work on so you can have success, but first and foremost to increase your faith that this can work for you too. You must believe in yourself enough and trust in your competence, resourcefulness, and grit to overcome whatever obstacles are before you in your entrepreneurial journey.

No matter what rejections or setbacks you face on your journey, your dreams, your why, your goals and your aspirations must carry you forward. There has to be a fire in you that wants to grow and wants to become more than what you are today. You have to develop an obsession for growth, that no matter what, nothing can stop you. You are already successful, it starts in your head. You must believe this about yourself in order for it ever to become reality. Our encouragement to you is to press on no matter the trials and the tribulations before you. Press on. You have it within yourself to accomplish more than any of the Agency Titans that have contributed to this book. All you have to do is decide that it's possible for you and that it's a reality for you and it's just a matter of time before it's realized.

So what do you do now? You take action.

Schedule a time to speak with us about the Limitless Agency Mastermind if you are ready to build a world-class, 7-figure marketing agency that lets you live life on your terms. Book your complimentary Limitless Agency Scaling Session with one of the Limitless Agency Coaches right here: **www.golimitlessagency.com**

Remember, your life is the sum of the decisions you've made up until this point. But the beautiful thing about life is that every single day, you have a new opportunity to take back control and build the life you want. It all starts with one simple decision. What happens next is up to you.

Franco Urbaez

Want us to help you build a 7-Figure Limitless Agency?

What if you could have an agency where the lead flow never stops, your dream clients stay for years instead of months, and your team handles the day-to-day so you can be what you've always wanted to be...?

The Owner.

Right now, you have a decision to make.

You could put this book down, satisfied with the knowledge you've gained, convinced that it's exactly what you needed to fix everything in your agency once and for all...

But who are you kidding?

In just a few days, like clockwork, you know that the momentum will die down and it'll be back to "business as usual".

And you'll be dealing with the same old problems, stuck in a vicious cycle of chasing the next deal, hitting the next deadline, making just enough money to get by and never enough to get ahead.

Throughout this book, you have learned from Agency Titans who have used proven strategies to earn 7 & 8-figures with their marketing agency and create a life of true financial freedom for themselves.

If you want to build a successful 7-figure marketing agency, there is no need to reinvent the wheel. The shortest path to success is to follow in the footsteps of those who have gone before you, to stand on the shoulders of Giants.

Take the first step on your path to financial freedom and schedule a free coaching call with a Limitless Agency Coach right now to get a personalized game plan to scale your agency to 7-figures in the fastest, easiest and surest way possible.

Don't leave your future up to chance, scan the QR code below and book your call now!

THE LIMITLESS AGENCY
www.golimitlessagency.com